'Sometimes you cry or laugh (
rarely do you experience all .... june's story is
deeply fascinating, challenging and impacting. I'm certain
that as you read you will discover a God who loves you; the
same Lord Jesus who is with June's family and also with you,
in every single circumstance.'
*Rev Anne Calver, author, speaker, church leader, Unleashed
overseer*

'This book is a beautiful story of love and loss, right and
wrong, and what we will do for the happiness of those we
love. Through the ups and down of life, June has trusted in
God. Her faith in Jesus is all that June needed for strength
and courage. I believe many people will benefit from reading
this book.'
*Millie O'Connor, Church Officer; Chair and founder of The
Millie's Foundation*

A Hand Stretched Across the Void

June Whitehouse

instant
ap◻stle

First published in Great Britain in 2023

Instant Apostle
104A The Drive
Rickmansworth
Herts
WD3 4DU

British Library Cataloguing-in-Publication Data

A catalogue record for this book is available from the British Library.

This book and all other Instant Apostle books are available from Instant Apostle:

Website: www.instantapostle.com

Email: info@instantapostle.com

ISBN 978-1-912726-68-4

Printed in Great Britain.

If I live, I get more time with my family here, and if I die,
I get time with my Father in heaven. What is there to be
afraid of?

Tracey June Greenaway

Contents

Foreword: 1982

I was crossing the line, drifting into a peaceful sleep, when I heard the phone ring. I looked at the clock on the bedside table. It was 12.30am. Who would be calling at this time of night? Irritated, I went downstairs and lifted the receiver, my sleepy ears still not prepared to hear the voice on the other end of the phone.

'Hello, this is the transplant coordinator at Queen Elizabeth Hospital.'

My heart started beating rapidly and an unexplainable swell of heat hit all parts of my body. I listened to the voice calmly inform me they had a kidney that was a possible match for Tracey! The voice asked me a series of questions about Tracey's health at that moment in time. The answers I gave ticked all the boxes and, after what seemed like a long silence, she advised me to bring Tracey to the transplant ward as soon as possible.

As I put the receiver down, my whole body was shaking. I felt intense excitement and overwhelming fear simultaneously about what this could mean for my critically ill sixteen-year-old daughter, who lay sleeping in her bed. I ran up the stairs two at a time to change out of my nightdress. My husband, Clive, was still in bed, anxiously waiting for me to say who was on the phone, but all I could do was simply shout, 'Hospital, it's a kidney, get dressed!' I rushed into the girls' bedrooms to wake them. In no time at all, we were in the car and on our way.

The corridors in the hospital were quiet, the lights were dimmed and all we could hear was the occasional sound of footsteps passing through the wards. A nurse greeted us after a while, with a kind, smiling face, and proceeded to guide us to a small waiting room.

After what seemed like hours of waiting, the nurse came bustling back, carrying a small tray of hypodermic needles, syringes and specimen bottles all to be filled with blood samples from Tracey, the small and frail teenager hoping for a second chance at life. We were then sent to the X-ray department to make sure that Tracey had no chest infection or fluid around her heart that could be problematic for surgery.

It was about this time that I remembered some concerns around Tracey's most recent blood results showing a very high urea count,[1] which was a worry. It might be owing to her medication needing to be assessed and changed.

I panicked and felt my blood pressure rise, knowing this could prevent her having this precious kidney; the past years had been so hard with many disappointments for my daughter, so it didn't feel right to say anything at that point. I decided it was best to wait to see what the surgeons found.

Prior to this, Tracey had been on haemodialysis for two years at home, which is a four-hour process (plus at least

---

[1] Meaning the kidneys weren't working very well.

an hour to set up beforehand and to sterilise and put everything away afterwards) where a machine removes, cleans and returns the body's blood; something her kidneys could not do. Her machine, when not in use, fitted neatly into a specially built wardrobe made by her uncle Jack, who was a carpenter. The wardrobe stretched from wall to wall across the room, taking up the largest portion of her bedroom. As well as her dialysis machine, it contained all the medical equipment that came with it, including hypodermic needles and sterile packs, bags of saline, haemodialysis blood flow lines, heparin bottles, line clamps, lignocaine[2] to stop pain and feeling around the area where Tracey put in her blood flow needles, surgical gloves and many more medical utensils. With all of this she was only left with a small space for clothing in the wardrobe. I can distinctly remember her bedroom always smelling of concentrate from the fluid that we had to mix with water and pour into the machine to start her treatment; the smell lingered on all her clothing, which was a constant reminder to us each day of her dialysis.

On dialysis days, the machine was pulled out of the wardrobe on its rollers and positioned at the side of her bed. She would have to inject herself with two needles to allow her blood to pass through the machine and back into her body; the whole process took five hours.

Tracey dialysed every Monday, Wednesday and Friday, and attended a clinic at hospital once or twice a month; how different her life was from that of most teenage girls. The dialysis was keeping her alive but giving her no quality of life. She could not live a normal

---

[2] A local anaesthetic.

teenage life, not only because of the dialysis itself but also because of the damage it was causing to her body. Knowledge of her condition in those days led doctors to believe that without further advancement in the medical field she would not live much past her teenage years.

However, at the age of sixteen, all this pain and suffering could come to an end with this transplant, this potential new lease of life that I had been hoping and praying for!

This was the start of the amazing story that was the life of Tracey June Greenaway, formally Tracey June Whitehouse, and her family. Please join me as I revisit the ups and downs of the woman who touched hundreds of lives, and how God has spoken to me as her mother and revealed Himself with miracles, healing and love along the way, extending His hand across the void for me to take hold of.

1
Early Years

My early years are the foundation and preparation for my journey, which started at the height of the Second World War.

I was born into an already overstretched family. I was the fifth child and certainly not planned! Like most families in those days, we had very little and lived each day making the most of what we did have.

Mum stayed at home to look after the family and Dad worked on heavy machinery, with long shifts in a local foundry; he was a hard man who always had to have the last word. Like many men in Dad's circle of friends, he spent much of his earnings on alcohol and often came home drunk and abusive to Mum. Unfortunately this was not an uncommon way of life back then.

The story passed to me over the years was that Mum met Dad in her late teens. She was never a strong person and suffered ill health throughout her very unhappy childhood and adult life. One day, Mum realised that she was pregnant, so she and Dad decided to get married in what I'm sure would have been a simple wedding.

After a few months of marriage, my brother Joseph was born, and as the eldest he saw most of the heartache and pain that Mum went through. Two years later, David was born, followed by their first daughter, Primrose Betty. Life by this time was getting difficult for Mum, as Dad was drinking and money was scarce. Another child came along, a third boy, Tony Anthony (although we called him Alf). By this time there were so many children that unfortunately not much attention was given to him. Imagine the frustration and pain Mum must have felt when she discovered that there was yet another unplanned child on the way! This time it was me, another girl, born on the 28th June 1941. The years of childbirth and hard work had taken their toll on Mum, and her health had started to deteriorate. However, there was to be a sixth and final child, Jean, who was born just eighteen months after me. So this was our family. Six children: three girls and three boys!

From an early age, I used to tag along with my brothers and their friends. I remember one occasion, when I was about five years old and it was bonfire night. Some of the youths had fireworks, but not the type you would see today; in those days there were few varieties, and our friends, who had little money, would mainly have sparklers. One of the boys threw a firework we called a 'Bengal match' into the air – it was the same as household matches, only longer and chunkier, and as it burned, it threw off all different colours. The firework had been thrown towards the sky and as it came down, it landed on the left side of my neck, lodging between my clothing and burning deep into my skin.

I was rushed to hospital and spent weeks in isolation. Hospital visits were limited in those days but, because of the seriousness of my condition, I was allowed extra visits. I had double pneumonia, followed by scarlet fever, and underwent skin grafts for my burns. The doctors held little hope that I would pull through all these complications. However, against all the odds, I returned home.

There was always sickness in our house when we were children. I suppose it came with the times when there was so much poverty, and medicine was not so advanced. I often wonder how Mum coped with all the illness and stress.

One day, my brother fetched me from school, and I could sense something was wrong. I overheard people saying 'TB' but I was only five and didn't know what that was. Initially, I didn't realise it was my mum they were talking about.

Some months later, owing to Mum's ill health, we moved from our small three-bedroomed home into a newly built four-bedroomed house in Oldbury, which is in the West Midlands. The house was huge, with a back garden that overlooked a farm, and for miles all you could see was fields. As children, walking to the bottom of the garden and climbing over the fence was the most wonderfully exciting experience on earth, with meadows and hills that stretched far into the horizon! During the day, cattle grazed at the bottom of the garden.

These were happy times. During the hot summer days, we would have great fun playing with our friends, building dens and getting into trouble with the farmer, who would often catch us scrumping his apples and chase after us with his stick. I loved to be outdoors playing with all my friends.

The area was lovely, with neighbours who used to sit on walls, chatting; they were good to us as they knew Mum was often ill in bed. They regularly rallied together to cook stews and puddings for us. However, one of the neighbours was not so sympathetic and she took a petition to all the houses in the road asking for signatures to get us evicted. She lived in one of the posh private houses and wanted us out because Mum had tuberculosis, and because we were scruffy kids playing in the street.

Our garden was a wonderland for us as kids. We had two ducks called Donald and Gobbles that swam in an old crock sink embedded in the soil that made a great pond. Roger, the brindle Staffordshire Bull Terrier, wandered freely all day, as did Billy the cat.

I loved the new house but hated the winters as they were long, dark and bitterly cold. The wind blew across the fields, whistling as it pushed through the gaps of the wooden sash cord-type windows. We never had any heating in the bedrooms; all we had was a coal fire in the living room. Dad used to open the oven door in the kitchen and turn on all the hobs. The kitchen would get lovely and warm, and as we walked down the stairs we could feel the heat. This would warm us up in the mornings before going out to walk the long journey to school. I don't remember ever seeing an electric fire. When we spoke, we could see the mist of our breath hitting the bitter air. Everything felt damp and smelled musty. There was as much frost on the inside of the windows as there was outside, and to see through, we had to scrape a little hole in the ice.

I shared a bedroom with my sisters Betty and Jean, which contained an old-fashioned dark wooden wardrobe that was so big we couldn't move it, an old chest of drawers and a chair that sagged in the middle. We had a double bed with a sprung mattress that dipped in the centre from years of wear, and the floor covering was lino that had patches of brown showing through the worn parts. At the side of the bed was a small homemade podged rug that Mum had made from old coats cut into small strips that were poked through a square piece of sackcloth.

Sometimes, in the evening, Dad would put a house brick in the oven to get very hot, wrap it in a towel and then put it in our bed; it was as good as a hot-water bottle. The three of us girls had to share the double bed, so we would argue over who would sleep in the middle, as that was the warmest place. In the winter we slept in jumpers, socks and anything else that could keep us warm.

Dad was very strict; from an early age we were never allowed to come downstairs unless we were fully dressed and ready for school. Dad always cooked a hot breakfast of thick, stodgy porridge, but when money was short, we had a 'noggin' of bread dipped in bacon fat, which we used to call 'licker' or a 'dip in the pon'.

When Dad was getting me ready for school in the winter months, he would put some of his old socks on my hands to use as gloves and pulled a double-sided scarf through its centre to serve as a hat.

One of the memories I still shudder at was never having good shoes; I always had second-hand shoes with holes in the bottom. I remember having to put pieces of cardboard or newspaper into the soles to try to keep my feet dry. I also remember putting two spare pieces in my pocket to replace the soggy ones when I got to school! The only time I ever remember having new shoes was for Sunday school anniversaries, when I had new, white sandals. Dad always sent us to Sunday school although he never went to church.

The night before a Sunday school anniversary, my aunty would put what we called 'rags' in my hair, and when she combed it the next morning it would fall into ringlets. These rags were long strips of material that she wrapped round sections of my long blonde hair, which stayed in overnight.

The church had a specially built platform that went up in rows so that every child could be seen. Jean and I were so proud, showing off our new white dresses. Some of the older children were given a poem to learn weeks before. The year it was my turn, I proudly stood up to say the poem I had learned. My dad was there, and seeing the proud look on his face as he clapped made it special.

After the anniversary service we would parade around the streets following the drumbeats and music from the Boys' Brigade or The Salvation Army. The church leaders would go round with buckets, collecting donations from those who were watching. When the service was over, Dad went to the pub, and Betty stayed at home to prepare and cook the dinner.

I never enjoyed my schooldays because the other children made it a hurtful experience. One day, while sitting at my desk, writing in my school notebook, a little creepy thing dropped out of my hair onto the page. It was the first time I had ever seen a head louse, which we called nits. Dad looked through my hair that evening and it was infested with lice. He rubbed a lotion into my scalp before combing it through. It had to be left on for two days without washing. The smell was awful. All the kids in class moved away from me and called me bug-yed (local slang for bug head!). It took ages to get rid of the smell because my hair was so long.

I have no real recollection of Mum being out of bed and cooking tea or making meals. Some days I came home from school and she was missing, and Dad would tell me that she was in hospital.

During her time of pain and suffering, and knowing that she was dying, her heart must have been breaking, knowing that she was leaving her children in the hands of Dad, who was so unequipped to look after six children. She must have spent hours imprisoned in loneliness and fear in her bedroom, agonising each day and night, wondering how we would all cope and what would happen to us.

I remember Dad holding Jean's and my hands when we visited Mum's grave. There was a gravestone with these words:

Farewell dear husband, my life is passed.
My love was true whilst life did last.
But now for me no sorrow make
but love my children for my sake.

These words must have encouraged Dad to press on.

The saying in those days was that children should be seen but not heard, and that was the case when it came to Dad. It may have been that he was so upset and could not cope with Mum's passing, but he made decisions that were not good for us children. I remember feeling afraid as I lay in bed at night, and many times I cried because I missed Mum so much. I still suffer at times with uncontrollable fear that makes my whole body ache and often turns into a full-blown panic attack. Dad was not understanding as he was struggling himself with the loss of Mum, and my brothers and sisters didn't seem to understand how it had affected me.

I often wonder how different my nature may have been if I'd had Mum's listening ear, her cuddles of love and her guidance as I grew up. I remember walking through the fields one day shouting, 'Mummy, Mummy, Mummy,' just to know what it felt like to say the word I could never say in my childhood.

Betty didn't have it easy with our brothers. As the oldest girl, she often came home from work and had to do the washing, which with our washing machine was no easy feat! The washer was manual, with a handle on the lid that we had to turn that allowed the paddles to beat the washing. We used carbolic soap to remove stains and our arms ached after only a few minutes of turning the handle. The wet clothes were then pushed through the rollers of a solid iron mangle that stood in the yard. It was about six feet high and, by turning a huge wheel on the side, the rollers turned and squeezed out excess water from the clothes, leaving them ready to put on the line. It amazes me that none of us ever had our fingers caught in that old mangle, as we were only children. It's surprising how quickly you learn when you have no choice.

The highlight of our childhood years was our annual two-week camping trip to Porthcawl in Wales. Dad would pack as much food and clothing as possible into a huge, battered old tin trunk that took two people to carry by holding a handle on each side. It also served as a seat when the train was full. We never had much money to spend on our holidays, but once we were there, we had the sea and the sand dunes, and we easily made friends to play with, so we still had a good time.

One day, we were playing in the sea when a huge wave pushed me off my feet and I started to drown. It was all very quick, and the next thing I knew, a big hand was pulling me to the surface. Dad always said it was my long hair that saved me. All my family and friends were searching for me in the dark, murky water when Dad felt something wrap around his ankle. He bent down to see what it was, and to his amazement it was my long blonde hair. Although close to death, I survived; that was the second – after the Bengal match incident – of many miracles!

So that was my early years. A mixture of pain, loss and deprivation, but all mingled with happy memories. Despite the problems, my family loved each other and there are fond memories that we can look back on. If only Mum had been with us to experience them too. These early years helped shape my character, which continued to be moulded throughout my teenage years.

2
All Grown Up

I left school in 1956, at the age of fifteen, with very little education and feeling like the class dunce. My school reports were always poor, but it didn't matter to me because I knew I was going to end up working in a factory. My first job was working on a steel tubular metal cutting machine called a lathe, which I didn't need any education for; all I needed was to work hard, and I certainly knew how to do that.

I wanted to put some of my first few weeks' wages towards buying myself a new bicycle. However, I knew Dad would have my pay packet and give me pocket money, so that wouldn't be an option. On my first morning at work, I felt so excited that I could hardly wait to walk through the factory gates, and I made sure I arrived well before the 'bull' sounded. We called it the 'bull' because it was a loud horn in the factory yard that could be heard for miles. It was the sign that work was starting, and we had three minutes to punch our clock card in the machine as we entered the gates. Back then, if we hadn't punched our clock card in the machine on time, we were locked out and missed half a day's pay, which was a lot of money!

Working on the lathes was hard and smelly work; sometimes the tubes were thick and as we cut through the metal with the cutting tool, slithers of hot swarf (hot strips of metal) would shoot off the cutting tool and stick on our face or arms, burning our flesh. The slurry oil was a white, milky kind of chemical that came from a small tube that poured over the cutting tool to cool the metal, but it didn't always cool it enough, and that's why it burned. After work we would all smell of suds oil; it was in our hair, in our clothes and on our skin, and my hands were always chapped and rough with the continuous soaking of the suds.

By this time, my brother Tony and I were close and always spent time together. We were the rebellious pair, with him being a Teddy Boy and me being a Teddy Girl. We enjoyed going to the local pavilion to dance. When I left the house and was far enough out of sight, I would pull out my make-up. It was the style to have thick pencilled eyebrows and heavy make-up with bright-red lipstick. I felt so grown up and independent wearing my make-up and flicking the end of my Woodbine cigarette, but I had to be home by 9.30pm. I didn't dare come home late, because Dad would come looking for me, and that meant trouble.

My brother David then started showing serious signs of illness. He became very lethargic and lost weight, making him look very pale and thin. His health deteriorated rapidly over a period of months until he was finally admitted to hospital.

After weeks of medical tests, the surgeons had to remove one of his kidneys. We were all pleased to see great progress following the surgery, as he seemed to be getting well again, and with medication he was allowed to come home. He looked so well, his colour came back into his cheeks and he put on weight.

I remember the day he came home; he was so happy – he had asked his girlfriend to marry him, and she had said yes. They had a wonderful wedding and they both looked radiant as we all gathered to wave them off for their honeymoon. However, the happiness was to be short-lived. It was just three months before he fell ill again. He sadly passed away with renal failure, after enduring months of operations and pain. He lost his fight for life the day after his twenty-third birthday.

Dad was a broken man from losing his son at such an early age and seeing him buried next to Mum; such unbearable heartache for any parent to have to endure.

After working for a few years at the factory on a variety of heavy machinery, I decided to look for new employment with a higher salary. My next job was at a factory that was closer to home, which was good in the winter as I always walked to work. While working, I had an accident on a power press that resulted in me losing the top of the first finger on my right hand. The machine had repeated and the guard had failed, so my hand was unprotected. I had never imagined you could feel so much pain from a finger.

After twelve months of fighting for compensation, I decided to leave factory work and started to look for another job; something new and different. I was surprised to be accepted as a petrol station attendant, a job I knew nothing about.

In the early 1960s, when you drove into a petrol station the attendant would put the petrol in your car, check the water in your radiator and top it up with antifreeze if needed, then check your oil and tyre pressures. There was no self-service. I loved working outside, meeting different people and being my own boss, so this job was perfect for me.

After a few weeks of working there I met my future husband, Clive. He worked as a driver. He came to the pumps for petrol and started a conversation, and twelve months later we were married.

Dad could never take to any of my boyfriends and made my love life difficult. He found fault with each one because he never wanted me to leave home.

On our wedding day it was like a battle zone. Not all my family liked Clive and I was not fully accepted by Clive's family. Clive's dad, though, made me feel so welcome. He was a wonderful and funny man who always played tricks. I'm reminded of the time he was walking home from work and some children said to him, 'Penny for the guy, mister?' Stan stopped, gave them a penny and walked off with their guy. The children chased him, calling for him to give it back. He smiled and handed the guy back with a few more pennies. He was such a funny and lovable person, and we quickly became close.

The first home Clive and I moved into was at the back of a hairdressing salon. We had a ground-floor living room and three bedrooms, but the downside was that we had to share our kitchen with the hairdressing staff. This meant we had to wait until the shop closed before we could prepare or cook any food. However, because we were both out at work all day, it was not a problem. We had no furniture other than a table that was given to us by family, so we would sit on the hairdressers' chairs after they had closed.

Like all newlyweds, we had the usual arguments. Our arguments always seemed to revolve around Clive's friends and money spent on smoking and drinking. I walked out so many times, shouting that I was never coming back, though I always knew I would because I had nowhere else to go! As the saying goes, I had made my bed so now I had to lie in it. I was in this marriage, so I would have to make it work.

Clive and I had to work together, and we had to make changes. We moved from the hairdressers' shop into our first rented house. However, after a few months we received a letter to say we would have to move yet again because of plans to extend the nearby motorway. Our house was the last one on the plans to be demolished, and because we were not on the council list, we would only be offered a high-rise flat.

3

A Growing Anxiety

Tracey June was born on my twenty-fifth birthday – 28th June 1966. I was full of a heavy cold and frightened to hold her in case I passed on my illness. I remember feeling so alone and afraid of making her ill; all I wanted was my mum to help me to be a mum! This little baby was totally dependent on me, and I was so unprepared.

After a few weeks, I started to settle into my new lifestyle of having a third person in the house. They were tiring days, with all the night feeds and the nappies to wash and keep spotlessly white. The nappies were pieces of square towelling, folded into a triangle shape and fastened in the front of the baby's tummy with a large nappy pin. This meant that every time the baby opened her bowels or passed water, her nappy needed to be changed. They were not like modern-day nappies. If not changed right away, the babies' bottoms became very sore.

This was a completely new life for Clive and me! Holding this baby quickly became such a joy each day. I remember feeling so proud as I pushed my new two-tone brown coach-built pram, with Tracey gurgling inside.

One sunny day, when Tracey was fast asleep in the pram, I walked past the church where I'd been to Sunday school during my childhood. However, the old building was no longer in use. They had built a new church right across the road. It all looked so different, as over the years the area had changed. A thought passed through my mind. I wanted to thank God for my lovely baby girl. I tried the door at the front entrance of the church. It was open, so I walked in and sat down for a while, just thinking over the past years. I can remember saying simply, 'Thank You,' for my daughter. At that time, I had not been to church for many years, but somehow it felt an amazing comfort to be there.

As the years passed, I began to have a feeling that something was not quite right with my little girl. I took her to the doctor several times and was told I was being overanxious, worrying over nothing. Tracey complained quite frequently of tummy ache and did not want to eat; she was often very lethargic and tired. Because I watched her daily, I could see these signs, but on taking her to the doctor she seemed to perk up, and so they probably thought I was a little neurotic. At times she looked so healthy that even I was puzzled. However, I could not overlook the fact that she struggled so often. I knew there was something medically wrong.

Over the following months, I was at the doctor's so often that the staff started to give me disapproving looks, which made me feel incompetent as a parent. Tracey, around five years old at this point, also struggled with bedwetting; the doctor gave me a book of sticky stars to give her each time she had a dry night. I was advised to wake her in the night to take her to the toilet. The doctor didn't seem concerned and acted as if stickers would fix the problem.

My second daughter, Vicky Teresa, was born just nineteen months after Tracey, and the two of them were so different. Vicky was so healthy. I couldn't count how many times her friends had to fetch Clive because she was stuck up a tree. I had never known a child to have so many cuts, bruises and accidents. The staff and nurses at our local Accident and Emergency department (A&E) knew Vicky by name and described her as a proper livewire. She was always in trouble, but she brought immeasurable joy to our lives.

We lived in the high-rise flat for about five years before we managed to exchange for a three-bedroomed council house in Dudley... quite a distance from our family and friends. However, we settled into our new home, and I loved it. Having a garden was especially great as it meant the children had somewhere to play.

I registered the family at a doctors' practice closer to our new home with a hope of a second opinion on Tracey's health. However, after several months, I realised that I was going to have another battle, as they too insisted that I was an overanxious mother. One of the doctors even implied, in front of Tracey, that I was at the surgery just as often as he was. This shocked and really upset me. I could understand their perplexity as Tracey seemed so well at times; however, she was also frequently ill, and this was not natural.

I decided to seek a third opinion. On the day of Tracey's appointment, I nervously sat in the surgery waiting room, waiting for Tracey's name to be called. As I entered the room, the doctor was reading Tracey's medical notes. I sat tensely and waited for him to finish. He asked me some questions and looked at Tracey. She was sitting next to me looking very healthy, irritably fidgeting because she didn't want to answer any of the doctor's questions. I tried to explain to him that this was one of her good days, that she often complained of tummy and back pains and that she was lethargic and often sickly.

The doctor looked at me with kindness and said perhaps I was overanxious. I was so upset and frustrated as yet again on the day the doctor examined her, she looked so well. How could I make them understand that she had so many symptoms that I could not explain?

In those days, what the doctor said was always right. You never questioned their decision; they were well respected, you listened to what they said and you had no legitimate retaliation. It was not like today. Suing a doctor was completely unheard of.

How could they not see that I had my second child, Vicky, who I rarely took to see the doctor? Surely that should have shown there was justification for my concern, otherwise my 'overanxious' behaviour would have been the same with Vicky.

After a while the doctors held a consultation, and I was prescribed antidepressants! By this time, I was beginning to think that it was me and perhaps I did need treatment because, after all, if you are told often enough that you are overanxious, then you begin to believe it.

If only there was someone I could talk to! I needed my mum; she would have been able to listen and help me. Clive had his work to worry about, and most of the time he had so many of his own pressures it was hard to talk to

32

him. I felt like my heart would not stop crying because I felt so alone and afraid in this new area, with no family or friends.

When Tracey started school, she thrived and really enjoyed it; she used to call her teachers 'Aunty' and they all loved her! Then, one day, the head teacher sent for me and confirmed what I had been saying for months. His words were, 'Mrs Whitehouse, your child is ill. We have been keeping a close eye on her and she is not eating. She is walking past the food counter and putting nothing on her plate, and we are very concerned.' I was quick to ask him to tell the doctors, as they would not listen to me.

The following day, I made an appointment to see the doctor with what I thought was the ammunition I needed from her head teacher. I was so disappointed when again the doctor simply said that Tracey was a little pale and prescribed her a tonic. I felt defeated, stupid and tired. I had explained to them time and time again that Tracey's symptoms were the same as my brother's, who had died at just twenty-three with renal failure, but they dismissed my thoughts and told me that renal failure was not hereditary. Years later I would find out that this, in some cases, is not true.

Tracey soon, quite understandably, became afraid of doctors. After all, she was becoming old enough to understand what they were saying, implying she was attention-seeking. Although she was only a child, she got the sense that they didn't believe her.

One day in the school playground, a ball hit her in the stomach. Although I knew it was not serious, I thought

33

this was a good opportunity to get her seen in A&E, so I took her to the local hospital. She was sent to be X-rayed and had water and blood samples taken, which came back showing blood in her urine. When the doctor said they were going to admit her, I immediately told them of my concerns, how the symptoms were similar to those of my brother who had died so young of renal failure. I told them that she would faint some days without warning, and about her poor appetite and lack of energy. I was relieved when the hospital said they would do some more tests. I finally felt listened to.

Tracey had been in the hospital for one week when the doctor stopped me on my way to the ward and told me I could take her home. I was devastated. That night in bed I started to think again, 'It must be me. The doctors are right!' The hospital wouldn't have sent Tracey home if she was sick, so I carried on taking the antidepressants. I became completely dependent upon them. My nature changed. I let myself go and I was tired most of the time. I lost my cheerful nature and became a complete nervous wreck.

After a while, it started to affect my relationship with Clive. We argued more often, and over a length of time he began to go out with his friends every night, drinking until after midnight, rather than be in the house with me. We were simply two people living separate lives in the same house. I think we both felt our marriage was over. I turned to my brother Tony for comfort and a listening ear.

One nice sunny morning, on the way home from dropping the children at school, I popped in to see a neighbour whose mother was on palliative care and had her bed downstairs in the living room. I stayed for a 'cuppa tea' and we chatted about many things, which helped to take my mind off my own troubles. The conversation turned to talking about older people in hospital who never had any visitors. She then shared her concern and fear that her mum's health had deteriorated very quickly, and how frail she had become.

I offered to sit with her mum and read to her, giving her daughter a break to go shopping. I loved to listen to her mum's stories of when she was young. I often pictured talking to my own mum and getting a feeling of comfort and a much-needed hug from her. I knew her mum loved to talk about the old times, so I would let her reminisce and just listen.

Some months later, as I was sitting listening to her mum, she turned to me and said, 'June, I'm slipping.' I thought she meant that she was sliding down her pillows, so I hugged her and lifted her back up, telling her that she was fine. She held my hand lovingly for a short while and then gave her last breath.

I was shocked and scared as it had all happened so quickly! Being alone with no phone in the house, I had to run to the neighbours next door to ask them to get help. When the doctor arrived, he told us it had been a massive heart attack and there was nothing that could have saved her.

That day made me ill for several months as I kept thinking, could I have done more for her? The doctor and her daughter tried to reassure me there was nothing I could have done, but for a long time I pictured her face and the desperation I had felt.

During the following months, my thoughts often returned to that conversation about older people in hospital who had no visitors. I started to think that maybe there was something I could do to help other people who were lonely or in similar situations to my friend's mother. I plucked up the courage and made a phone call to Burton Road Hospital, Dudley, and asked the matron for permission to visit the older people twice a week during the morning. She was delighted and said yes, I could!

After only a few visits to the hospital, the patients started to call me by name, and it was a good feeling to simply sit and talk with them. I felt I could speak to some of them as if I were talking to the mother I'd never had; they were a great comfort to me. I was visiting them, but the rewards I received on every visit far outweighed anything I could give them. The joy of supporting them benefited me more than any medicine. If any of them had a birthday, I would take them a bunch of flowers and some mint humbugs; they were always very popular with the patients!

Some of them wanted to talk while others wanted me to write letters for them. This was hard for me as my spelling was very poor, but I did my best and we often laughed as I asked them how to spell various words. Some of the letters were sad and filled with messages to family and friends they had fallen out with or lost contact with over the years. On taking the letters to the matron to post, she often said that relatives could not be traced or had passed away. However, I knew the patients felt better for putting in writing all that they longed to say to their loved ones.

I know now that Jesus had stretched out His hand and guided me to that hospital, to allow me to give the love I had within me. I was on a new journey at a pace I could cope with, by giving to others and enjoying receiving from them.

4
The Leaflet

One day, while I was shopping in Dudley town centre, a short Afro-Caribbean lady popped a leaflet into my hand. I glanced briefly at the leaflet before looking around, but she seemed to have disappeared. As I pushed the leaflet into my shopping bag, I noticed the headline 'Trevor Dearing Healing Service' across the top of the page.

Later, as I was putting my shopping away at home, I came across the leaflet again. This made me curious, as Tracey's health was always on my mind. I read the leaflet in more detail and found a contact number inviting people to book a seat on a coach to the next event, to listen to the Church of England evangelist and speaker Trevor Dearing. Maybe it was curiosity or maybe it was desperation, but either way it wasn't long before my coat was back on and I found myself walking to the phone box at the top of the road. I called the number and booked a seat for the evening venue.

When Clive came home from work, I asked if he would watch the children, as I was going out. He was surprised that I had booked to go on a coach at night, as it was something I would not usually do. That evening, several times after leaving the house, I felt like turning back.

I could see the coach at the pick-up point already waiting. Nervously, I climbed the first step onto it – and was amazed at the happy, loving welcome. It was fashionable at the time for ladies to wear a headband with a flower placed on the top; the coach seemed to be full of flowery heads. I found myself an aisle seat and told myself not to be nervous, because this was just the same as sitting on a bus when going shopping with strangers. I had nothing to be nervous about.

I was looking down, deep in thought about what could be ahead, when a voice said, 'Hello!'

I lifted my eyes to see a very tall, well-built man who had a kind face. I could almost see the radiance coming from him! He was Pastor Gerald Chamberlain. I didn't know it at the time, but this coach trip was going to completely change my life.

When we arrived at the town hall, the meeting had already started. I remember walking down the centre aisle and looking up to the balconies that were full of people standing with outstretched hands, singing with love and joy on their faces. Pastor Chamberlain had pre-booked the seats for the event and, surprisingly, there was an aisle seat for me at the end of a row. I had a fear of people sitting both sides of me and I know now that God had a plan for me to be there, even down to the details of my seat.

I was sitting four rows from the front when Trevor Dearing came on stage. This was the man I had come to listen to and, as I looked into his eyes, he completely captured my thoughts; my fears had gone. He talked about the apparent foolishness of God: about the story of

David from the Bible – how a young boy could kill a giant with a slingshot and a small pebble. He spoke too about how the Israelites walked around the walls of Jericho for seven days and on the seventh day blew trumpets and gave a loud shout, bringing the walls crumbling down, allowing them to win the battle. He talked about the parting of the sea and the people of Israel walking through on dry ground. I had heard all these stories before in Sunday school, but had never dwelt on them. They had never had any impact on my heart, until now.

Trevor finished his message by saying that only God could use these foolish things and make them work. He said that God loved us all and looked at our hearts, rather than at our mistakes or weaknesses.

After he had finished talking, he called for all those who were sick to come down to the front for prayer. I could hear seats banging all around me as people stood up and started to come down from the balconies. It seemed that the whole building was on the move. I was on the end of the row and so people were stood right next to me – there must have been hundreds of people.

Trevor asked the congregation to reach out their hands over these people and pray for all of them. I remember him saying, 'It's not me, Trevor Dearing, who heals, but it is Almighty God the Father who heals, and we are all going to ask for the healing of these people.' I had never prayed for anyone before, but I found myself praying for other people, complete strangers who were unwell. I didn't understand the words coming out of my mouth, yet they felt wonderful. My body was tingling and a warm swell seemed to comfort me. I felt lifted, excited, peaceful and strangely happy all at once.

The evening came to an end at around 10pm. I boarded the coach for the journey home to the pick-up point. We arrived back at around 11pm. From there I had to walk home as the buses had finished running for the night. Strangely, I cannot remember that walk, nor do I remember feeling any fear. I knew I was different; something had happened within me at this meeting, and I wanted to tell the world about it. I also really wanted to know more.

I asked Clive if I could go again the following night. I also asked my friend to come with me. She said she enjoyed it, but I am not sure if it had the same impact on her as it did on me.

The lady who handed me that leaflet when I was shopping will never know of the change she brought to my life or of the seed she had planted. When I look back, it was like an angel guiding me to a safe place where I met Pastor Gerald Chamberlain, the shepherd who nurtured me and brought me into a church full of loving, caring people. I never felt alone again, and I had plenty of shoulders to cry on – people who truly cared. The loving church family prayed for me, and showed me the power of prayer. They taught me how to seek Jesus, the Son of God who gave His life for me on the cross and paid the price for my sin. I wanted to know the journey Jesus walked, and all about the Holy Spirt.

The Lord not only changed me, but amazingly, He also saved my marriage. Clive and I began to enjoy being together again.

Twelve months later, I was baptised by my wonderful pastor, and from that day I was no longer the same person. I found my self-confidence and self-worth; I had a joy in my heart each morning instead of anguish. I woke with a 'Good morning, Lord!' and prayers. I had been stripped of confidence and I had felt alone, but God had seen my every tear.

It seemed He had set the plan in action at the right time, with the visiting of the older people in hospital, the leaflet, the coach, even to the end-of-row seating, and the church family. He had been preparing my new season and next journey.

5
Diagnosis

Tracey was twelve when we moved back to Oldbury, to the place where I had grown up, near the fields that I had played in as a child. It felt so good to move back home, closer to my family. The exchange process, overseen from one borough council to another, was so quick that I knew it was answered prayer. I had to go through the traumatic thought of leaving my church family, and that frightened me a little, because they had carried me through so much over the past years.

Pastor Chamberlain was sad to see me go but reassured me that he would still be there for me when I needed him. On my final morning service, I was presented with a book of daily readings that I still treasure to this day. Pastor Chamberlain did his best to make sure I had good spiritual guidance when I left his church. He introduced me to two inspiring people to guide me through my next journey. Pastor Arthur Colman and his wife, Ivy, were pastors of the Pentecostal Holiness Church, closer to my new home.

Tracey and Vicky loved the new church and enjoyed making new friends in the youth group.

It was during these years that Tracey and Vicky were baptised, but the church we attended did not have a baptism pool. The pastor arranged for the service to be held at Tame Road King's Community Church – it was the sister church to George Road Community Church, which we attended. We were unaware at the time of God's planning, but this day was going to play a big part in all our lives.

Tracey and Vicky were baptised by Pastor Colman, alongside others in the youth group. It was a joyful day shared with all the family. The two girls, surrounded by all the youth, were so excited. It was so delightful to see such joy and love for the Lord.

When we were settled in our new home, I had to register at the local surgery. I was surprised to see the wife of the doctor who had treated my brother David before he died of renal failure in 1953! Sadly, her husband had passed away. I remember him with such fond memories, for his kindness in those final days of David's life. She had no recollection of my family, but I was pleased she had taken charge of the surgery. I thought I might feel more relaxed talking to a female doctor, making it easier to stress my anxiety and fears; I thought perhaps she might be more understanding.

On our first visit she looked at Tracey's records and I noticed her face change as she read the comments from previous doctors. Computers were not around in those days, so when we visited a doctor, the reason for the visit and medication were written on a card, pushed into a brown envelope and filed in boxes marked with a surname. Tracey's envelope was bulging with cards because of the number of past visits.

I felt uncomfortable waiting for the doctor to read through the comments. After a short time of asking Tracey questions, she said, 'Mrs Whitehouse, don't you know your daughter is going through puberty?'

I felt my whole body cry out, 'Oh please, not again!' All I wanted was a new perception of what could be wrong! Tracey was in tears as we walked home with no medication and feeling so poorly; she felt yet again she was being accused of attention-seeking.

After three weeks she was no better, so again we went to see the doctor. As soon as I entered the waiting room, I experienced that same uncomfortable feeling. I sat waiting for our name to be called, worrying that the doctor was going to say there was nothing wrong again. However, this time I really was anxious! Tracey had been so ill with so many strange symptoms. I was really at the end of my tether. I needed help and answers.

In the end, I said, 'My daughter is ill! And I don't enjoy wasting my time sitting in your waiting room.'

The doctor looked at me, shocked. I was also shocked! There was tension in the room as the doctor examined Tracey and asked her if she could do a water sample. And then, looking at the sample, the doctor's face changed. She said, 'Tracey has sugar in her water; that is not a good sign.'

I blurted out, 'At last! You agree that there is something wrong!'

The doctor was very apologetic and arranged for an appointment to be made to see a paediatrician consultant at Dudley's Guest Hospital.

This appointment was the start of a long and painful journey for all the family, one that would span a little more than two decades. On our second visit, in 1978, the consultant at the hospital said he had received all of Tracey's test results. Clive and I knew that it was not going to be good news. However, nothing could have prepared us for what we were about to hear.

The consultant held his hands slightly raised and said, 'I am sorry, but it's too late, there's nothing left, there's nothing we can do for Tracey.'

My thoughts were, 'Oh please no, Lord, my little girl is going to die!'

The consultant looked concerned and said how sorry he was that it had gone this far. He proceeded to tell us that Tracey was a very poorly girl and had kidney failure. Her symptoms were hard to detect because she was still passing urine, which was unusual for renal failure. He told us that Tracey had Bright's disease (which was hereditary), and we finally had answers.

Little was known about Bright's disease, nephritis[3] or chronic renal failure in those early days; today it would have been detected quickly, especially in Tracey as she had shown many of the symptoms. We were told Tracey needed to undergo surgery for a ureteral reimplantation.[4] The consultant called East Birmingham Hospital[5] to book an appointment and assured us that he was sending us to the best renal paediatrician in the country.

---

[3] Kidney inflammation.
[4] To replace the tube to the kidney.
[5] Now Heartlands Hospital.

On our first meeting with the doctor at the Birmingham Children's Hospital, I felt at ease and just knew he was the best. He said he would carry out an operation that might keep Tracey off dialysis for a year, but by now it was like shutting the stable door after the horse had bolted. This operation had only recently been pioneered and was made to correct kidney reflux by creating a new tunnel, changing the way the ureter[6] connects to the bladder.

During the latter part of 1978, Tracey was admitted into the Birmingham Children's Hospital, and for several weeks she was *very* poorly. She had tubes coming from her tummy, a catheter was fitted and she was connected to all kinds of monitors and machinery following the operation.

Some weeks later, when the catheter was removed and each tube into her tummy was taken out, Tracey went to the toilet for the first time in weeks. Because of the new connectives the surgery had made, it was very painful for her. I could hear her screams from the other end of the ward.

This was the first of many stays in the children's hospital. On one occasion, she was admitted to hospital for treatment on her teeth; she had stitches in her gums as her teeth were falling out because of her condition. She also developed what was called renal rickets. It was on this occasion that Roger De Courcey, who was a famous ventriloquist at the time, came to visit her and brought his puppet, Nookie Bear. Her picture was in all the local newspapers showing her swollen lips and face from the operation, but she still managed a smile. She was also paid a visit, while on dialysis, by Sarah Greene from *Blue Peter*,

[6] Tube that carries urine to the bladder.

who was researching for a programme about children who suffer with renal failure. Tracey loved meeting these people and they brought a welcome smile to her face in times of hardship.

JAN 22 1980

TEENAGER Tracey Whitehouse was feeling down in the mouth at Birmingham Children's hospital until she had a surprise visit from her favourite bear.

Tracey, aged 13, had to have two teeth pulled out at the hospital.

The youngster from Cookley Fay, on the Lion Farm Estate in Oldbury, has a kidney disease which means regular hospital visits, even for simple problems like taking care of her teeth.

But her most recent operation couldn't keep the smiles away when TV and pantomime star Roger de Courcey brought Nookie

Tracey gets a bear hug

Roger, who is appearing in Babes in the Wood at the Birmingham Hippodrome, made a surprise visit to cheer up youngsters on the wards.

And Nookie had a special hug for Tracey, who has been in and out of hospital for the past two years and

games like her classmates, Tracey's mother, June Whitehouse, said afterwards: "It was just the tonic Tracey needed.

"Her face lit up when Nookie arrived and it was like being with a different girl. She was laughing making jokes, and it made her day."

A newspaper article covering Roger De Courcey visiting Tracey in Birmingham Children's Hospital.

48

Tracey meeting Sarah Greene while dialysing at East Birmingham Hospital.

6
Dialysis

Smiling through pain was something that Tracey became known for. She inspired many of the other young people on the wards.

Through all these hospital visits and stays, I had wonderful support from my church family. They were there for me day and night, and Pastor Chamberlin (who kept in touch) often ferried us in his car to and from hospital, and paid Tracey regular visits at home. The church fellowship lifted me with prayers and stood by me on my good and bad days; they always understood and supported me.

When Tracey was coming to the end of the year's grace after the operation to delay the start of dialysis, she became poorly. The consultant said she needed to start dialysis. Clive and I received an appointment to attend the Paediatrics Renal Unit at East Birmingham Hospital. We were asked to come alone for our first visit to see the procedure of haemodialysis – using a dialysis machine.

The children on the ward were all quite small for their ages; some of this was owing to their condition of renal failure. There were about eight of them, waiting for their machines to be set up. Something drew my eyes to one little boy, who I thought to be about eleven years old, sitting on a chair beside his bed. The chair looked huge because he was so small. I glanced at him while trying not to let him know I was looking. I noticed he had a tourniquet in his hand and, to my amazement, he pulled the tourniquet tightly around the top of his arm. Not wanting to stare at him, I tried to look out of the corner of my eye. He reached to a tray on the bedside table and picked up a hypodermic needle with two clear plastic tubular lines fixed to the tail part. He pushed the needle into a vein in his arm and blood immediately started to flow through one side of the plastic lines. I was amazed to see the thickness of the needle – the tip looked like a matchstick. I was to find out that it was much thicker than the type used for a normal injection as the blood must flow through the machine quickly.

A nurse was there to assist him, but he put the needle in by himself. The nurse then wrapped micropore tape around the needle to keep it in place. The blood flowed through one side of the needle, around the lines and through the dialyser, the false kidney, which was fitted to the machine, and then flowed back through the second line back into his arm. I was so shocked. I never thought about all of this when the doctors mentioned dialysis.

I looked at Clive and noticed he had gone very pale. The ward sister must have noticed as she quickly ran over to assist him. The reality of dialysis began to permeate our thoughts. I glanced back at the boy and watched the nurse complete the procedure by setting the controls on his machine. He then lay back and started to eat a packet of crisps. The ward sister explained that patients are allowed treats for the first hour of dialysis, which could be a packet of crisps, a small handful of nuts or a few squares of chocolate. Any food that contains potassium is a great danger to renal patients if consumed after the first hour of dialysis, or any time during the week, so this short window of time to enjoy something normal was a treat.

We left the hospital that day feeling very afraid, confused and wondering how we would cope in the future.

A few weeks later, Tracey needed to start dialysis. She first had an operation to create a fistula, which is done by connecting an artery to a vein under the skin. This increases the pressure of the blood flow, allowing the vein to become stronger and larger for the patient to insert the needle. Because of the speed with which the blood rushes through the fistula, Tracey's arm would 'buzz', which you could feel and hear.

After the operation, Tracey started dialysis three days a week. Her arm was black with bruises from top to bottom through continuous needling; however, the doctors said that the skin would harden after a while, and she would not bruise so badly.

The following weeks brought many sleepless nights and tears. It was hard to accept and watch our daughter go through this painful procedure every other day, knowing that this would be her life until she had a transplant. After a while, we started to settle into the routine as part of our lives, and we knew dialysis could never be missed, not even if she was seriously ill. She would die if she missed her treatment.

Tracey made friends on the ward, and we became like a little family. Each mother would share emotions and tears, and if one of the children was seriously ill, we all kept in touch and supported each other.

The hospital transport arrived at 6.30am Mondays, Wednesdays and Fridays to collect us. The journey to the hospital took about an hour if there was no traffic. When we arrived at the renal unit, we had to wait for the nurse to set up Tracey's machine. Sometimes, if they were having a bad day, we would wait longer, and when that happened Tracey would start to fidget and get stressed, waiting to have her needles put in. Sometimes we could wait an hour before they came to fetch us from the waiting area. During this time, we would find things to do.

The nurses on the ward often played fun tricks on Tracey, and so one day Tracey thought she would pay them back. We both giggled as she wrote a fun poem about the nurses while waiting for her machine to be set up. Here's an extract:

> Every Monday Wednesday and Friday,
> I sit down quietly and pray.
> To ask the Lord to guide me,
> Every minute of the day.
>
> When I arrive at the unit,
> the nurses all curtsy and say,
> 'Come on Tracey dear,
> we haven't got all day.'
>
> All of them are needle-happy,
> Unless it's in their own vein.

Straight in and up they go,
No matter what the pain.

So, when you read this poem,
It's wrote [sic] with love and grace.
Thanks for all you do for me,
Great big thanks from Trace.

Once connected to her machine, the treatment lasted four hours. It would take even longer if the blood in her lines clotted or if she had a lot of fluid to remove. When her dialysis had finished, it used to take ages to stop the bleeding as the needles were in a main artery.

The final part of the treatment was filling in her medical notes by recording her pre-dialysis blood pressure, fluid intake, temperature and the post-treatment results.

Dialysis days were long, and we always felt completely wiped out! Hospital transport also took patients out of our area, which made the journey longer, making it even later when we arrived home.

Tracey's treatment was keeping her alive, but the process also made her ill. Dialysis in those early days of kidney research was harsh, and it took a toll on the mind and body; she was often tired, pale and lethargic between treatments. Clive was also under stress because he had to be at home for when Vicky came back from school, as most days I would still be at the hospital with Tracey.

Tracey's diet was extremely strict. Everything had to be weighed and all her vegetables had to be boiled in a large pan of water for a few minutes, then the water thrown away and the vegetables boiled again in fresh cold water. This process had to be done three times to remove all the potassium from the vegetables. She could not eat the same food as we did as all her food had to be specially prepared. I had to cook everything separately, keeping records of times, weights and quantities, even down to how many spoonsful of gravy I put on her plate, because of her fluid restrictions. This also included ice cream.

Life had changed. The pressure was so great, and looking back I sometimes feel I failed the rest of the family, especially Vicky. I should have given her more attention and consideration of her feelings. For instance, when we met friends or family, they always asked how Tracey was but never mentioned Vicky. It was tough on my younger daughter; it was tough for us all.

After months of dialysing at hospital, we were given the option to train for home dialysis. I was not very keen to do this as I was afraid, but the nurses assured me that it would be better for Tracey. I could see, too, that there were a lot of patients for them to deal with; having home dialysis would surely lighten the load. Anyway, regardless of their reasons, to please everyone I reluctantly agreed.

Clive's boss allowed him the occasional Friday off to train with me at the hospital. Clive was my support. We leaned on each other; he needed to know how to set up the machine in case I was ever too ill to do so, or incapacitated in some way.

For the first week of training, we were put in a side ward. Tracey was taught how to put her own needles in (at the age of fourteen) and I was taught how to hold my fingers on the vein and put cotton rolls of packing under the needle to keep a good blood flow. I hated the throbbing feeling of blood flowing through the vein, but I had to get used to it.

Once we had been shown what to do, we were left alone in a side room. We had to start and complete the treatment as if we were at home. We were not allowed to call for help unless we were in real trouble; we were reminded several times during our training that the nurses would not be on call at home. For this reason, we needed to be able to cope with every emergency, from the breakdown of the machine to Tracey passing out, and blood clotting in the lines.

My faith and love for Jesus was strong in those days. He gave me immeasurable strength and self-control. I was in the kitchen on the ward one day making a cup of tea, when one of the mothers commented that she could not understand how I could always be so happy and cheerful with all the pressure. I knew that my faith and trust in the Lord was helping me through, and that the nervous wreck had been transformed into a God-trusting, bold new person. I had stopped taking antidepressants when we found out that Tracey was indeed ill and that I was *not* an overanxious mother!

I was approached again about my cheerful attitude by the same mother a few days later . I shared my past with her and how I had found new life in Christ. I shared how the Lord had stepped into my life through the giving of a simple leaflet. She was amazed, and it really touched my heart when she said she wanted what I had. It was to be many years later, owing to a newspaper cutting and a phone call, that I would find out the impact of that conversation on the ward – she and her husband were pastoring a new church in the local area!

After many months of training, the day came when we were ready for home dialysis. We could dialyse any time – morning, afternoon or evening – but the treatment had to be every other day. This gave us more flexibility as we wouldn't have to travel to and from the hospital every dialysis day, saving us at least two hours. It also meant that I had more time with Vicky, which I was so thankful for. Vicky was getting older, and I felt a growing distance, so I tried to include her on dialysis days by asking for her help.

Vicky always tried to keep Tracey company on her treatment days as they enjoyed listening to music together. It was a joy to hear them both singing and giggling while playing board games. We often had the house full of young people from school and church; they would come to play their guitars and spend time with the girls. Many of our visitors passed comment on what a happy house it was.

On dialysis days, our routine was to start early in the morning and then Tracey could sleep in the afternoon, as the treatment left her weak and tired. Despite the six months of training, it was still very scary each time I put her on the machine. I felt afraid in case I had overlooked something while preparing the lines and pressures on the machine, which could have made Tracey very ill or even killed her. Some days I was full of confidence, and other days I was very nervous.

The mornings started with sterilising the machine and then mixing a solution called 'concentrate' with water. There were two sets of lines, one with red labels and one with blue labels, called arterial and venous lines. One drew the blood out, carried it through the false kidney and back into what we called the 'bubble trap' which disposed of any air that may have accumulated in the lines. The blood would then pass through the second line and back into Tracey's body. The false kidney in the machine did what healthy kidneys do every minute of the day in a normal person. For renal patients, their blood is only cleaned during that four-hour window when they dialyse, which means that for the rest of the time there are poisons being leaked into the bloodstream.

While I was setting up the machine, Tracey weighed herself to see how much fluid she was carrying following her last dialysis. When you have kidney failure you do not pass urine at any time, meaning that all fluids stay inside of your body, which is very dangerous. Dialysis removes this fluid.

Tracey prepared her tray on the tubular table supplied by the hospital and unwrapped the sterile pack that held her needles, syringes and clamps. She always prepared her own needles. Her fragile hands would shake as she pushed through the skin to first inject herself with lignocaine infusion anaesthetic. This first injection was put just under the skin in the area she would put her dialysis needles into her fistula, helping to numb some of the pain. She needed to make sure she had a good blood flow by inserting the needle in the centre of the vein, and then connect herself to the machine. Her face would show the pain, but she amazed me how she did it anyway. It was important during this time to take her blood pressure and check that all lines and pressures on the machine were set correctly. I also had to check that the bag of saline solution was put on the stand, in case her blood pressure dropped, which could happen through her dialysis. All this preparation would take about an hour before she even started her four hours of treatment.

There were mornings when Tracey had mood swings owing to her condition. She was a fourteen-year-old who wanted to do what her friends did. Some days she would refuse to go on her machine, which we both knew would be fatal. There were times she was so depressed it was hard to keep her spirits up.

When Tracey started home dialysis, I received an appointment to see a psychiatrist, which I was surprised about. On querying the appointment, I was told that it was normal procedure to help mothers to cope with the treatment of children who are on home dialysis. At first, I was sceptical; however, on my first visit I found the psychiatrist to be helpful as she understood how worried I was. I was pleased the renal doctor had made the arrangement for me to see her.

During the early months of dialysis, Clive and I asked if we could be tested to see if we were compatible to give Tracey one of our kidneys. Clive's results came back as negative, but mine were compatible! The transplant surgeon explained that there were still many tests to go through, and it's fair to say that at the time doctors were not happy about live donor transplants, as the success rate was not good and there were a lot of risks. The fields of transplantation, medication and dialysis machines in the 1970s and 1980s were in their early stages, but new treatments were being developed.

After what seemed like months, the initial tests started, and after still more months a date was set for the transplant to go ahead for Tracey to have one of my kidneys. Then we received the telephone call at 12.30am. The transplant coordinator said they had a kidney that may be compatible for Tracey, who was now sixteen years old. This was just days before our scheduled admission date.

We were to find out years later that God had different plans for my kidney, and His timing was perfect!

7
Walking in Trust

We had rushed to the hospital and were sitting in the waiting room for all the pre-operation tests to be completed. While we were in the waiting room, one of the nurses passed by and I asked if she knew how long it would be before the operation. She said they were still waiting for the kidney to arrive from Bristol.

It was a long night's wait as the operation was not carried out until the next morning. I was so excited and happy as I waited for Tracey to come back from theatre; my mind was full of how this kidney was going to change our lives and give Tracey, now sixteen, the normality of life she had never had. Images of her with rosy cheeks eating crisps and chocolate, having space for clothes in her wardrobe instead of a dialysis machine, kept my mind occupied while the surgeons worked.

However, as soon as we saw her after the operation, I knew there was something wrong as there were nurses and doctors all around the bed. We quickly learned that the kidney was not working properly and were asked to wait in the corridor. A few moments later the ward doors opened, and Tracey was being rushed back to theatre to have the kidney removed.

Tracey was very poorly for days following the operation, both physically and mentally. The doctors grew concerned about her, and even though she was recovering from the operation, she still had to go through the pain of four hours of dialysis every other day. I watched her day by day start to give up the fight. She refused food and drink and rarely opened her eyes. She didn't want to talk and so I would just sit with her during the day, holding her hand and waiting for a response.

At night, I slept in the nurses' quarters. I usually tried to stay by her bed until she was asleep and then I ventured to my room. To get to it, I had to walk along an awfully quiet basement, like a tunnel. I never liked that walk late at night as the corridors were eerie.

The first night I lay in bed with my thoughts racing and thinking of Vicky. Was she OK? Was she missing me? Was she crying? I felt so alone and so helpless. There were no mobile phones then, so it was difficult to get in touch with my husband.

I remember one night, it must have been about 1.30am. Tracey was poorly and in so much pain that it was unbearable for a mother to watch. She looked so small in that hospital bed and all I wanted to do was take her pain away, but there was nothing I could do. That night, I once again walked that tunnel back to my room in the nurses' quarters, then collapsed on the bed and started angrily beating the stuffing out of the pillow! *Why? Why? Why?* I was crying out and shouting to the Lord at the top of my voice. I felt God had let us down; why did this transplant fail? Why were we given hope, just to have it snatched away so quickly? All my church family were praying. This news would be such a disappointment to them and my family.

When I had cried for what seemed like hours, a picture started to form in my mind, like a vision.

I could see what looked like a straight road stretching into the distance; at the end of the road was a T-junction with a sign pointing to the right: 'Follow and trust Me.' To the left it said: 'Walk in anger without Me.'

It was hard for me alone in that room. However, I knew that from that moment, whatever happened, I wanted to walk with my Lord Jesus, trusting Him, as without Him there was nothing. I cried out, 'I choose to follow You, Lord. I choose to trust You. You are the only way for me.' In my heart I knew He would never leave us; He would watch over my little girl even while she lay in so much pain. He would always fight in her corner. I had to trust Him. After all, He knew her future; I did not.

Some weeks later, Tracey was moved from the hospital where she had had the transplant and transferred back to East Birmingham Hospital, where she dialysed to finish her recovery. She was put on a specific ward that would meet her dietary needs for her renal failure. She lay motionless in her bed, full of depression, not speaking to anyone and often refusing food. There were older patients on the ward who showed their concern and often tried to talk to her. It was such a hard time for Tracey. However, all was about to change. Once again, the Lord had His hand on her.

The youth group from our church in Oldbury (Pastor Colman's church) were such a happy, loving and caring group who were always playing practical jokes on each other. One day, they turned up at the hospital with their guitars at visiting time to see Tracey, but there were so many of them that they couldn't all get into the ward. Tracey's ward was on the ground floor and the young people were determined to see her. They made their way outside and stood in the grounds, looking through the open windows. The other patients on the ward were deeply moved by the love they all showed. The youth group started playing their guitars and singing for Tracey, with many of the patients joining in, and before long Tracey was sitting up in bed and her emotional recovery began.

I thank God for that act of love from those young people. I have always said that the church youth group woke her up and made her smile again. The other patients on the ward were asking if they would come back, and, of course, they did. The youth group was like a little family of God's children.

There was one special friend Tracey met at the youth group who was like a brother to her and a son to me – Sean. He walked with her every day through all her battles, and when he married Rose in 1983, she also loved and cared for Tracey. They were two very special people in her life. Sean and Tracey would laugh and cry together; the bonds they built were truly special and treasured by them both.

Tracey eventually came home, and we started the awful task of home dialysis again. This time, however, it was worse because Tracey was so poorly, and mentally drained. She had terrible mood swings and just wanted to

Tracey with Sean.

be a normal teenager. That phone call saying a kidney was available had filled her with hope for a short time, but that hope had now disappeared.

After a few weeks of being at home, there was yet another setback. The doctors told us that Tracey was too ill at this time for another transplant, and they were going to remove her name from the transplant list. These are the words that no patient or parent wants to hear. If you're not on the transplant list then all you have to look forward to is a life of dialysis, which made Tracey even more depressed. This news, during the long, fearful nights when everything seemed at its darkest, made me recall what the doctor had said several years earlier, implying she may not live past her teens.

Over time, she started to act like herself again and I saw that sparkle of life come back into her eyes. Tracey had picked herself up, even against all the hardship and pain she was suffering. This ability to pick herself up was something she was to become known for later in life.

Tracey and Vicky were two incredibly special girls, and when the two of them were together, there was no telling what might happen. The house was never empty of young people, and everything was fun. We *chose* to work at making everything fun, especially on dialysis days. The girls were forever playing jokes on me. Even while Tracey was on the machine, it didn't stop her!

Tracey was allowed a small portion of pizza during the first hour on dialysis, so when she was settled and all her medical records had been written down, I would pop downstairs to put her thin-based homemade pizza under the grill. On many occasions when I walked away from the machine, the alarm would sound, indicating that something was wrong. I had to charge up the stairs two at a time to correct the fault. Countless times, I forgot about the pizza until smoke came drifting into the bedrooms. With the amount of smoke coming out of the open windows, passers-by probably thought the house was on fire. This was a standing joke for many years. It was only by hearing the girls giggling after several times of it happening that I found out they were playing a trick on me; Tracey made the machine sound the alarm on purpose by clamping one of the lines just to trick me and have me running up and down the stairs. They thought it was hilarious!

One day we received a visit from an old friend who had travelled from London with his three children. It was on a dialysis day, so his children sat on the floor in the bedroom watching the process and didn't mind the blood in the lines or the sound of the machine. After a little while I looked at the children's father, who was sitting on the only chair in the bedroom. I noticed the colour had drained from him just as he keeled over and passed out. I was busy getting him water while all the children found it quite funny.

My sister Jean had started to visit me on dialysis days. She came to give me support and I really looked forward to her company. Some days when there were problems, her presence just helped keep me calm. During Jean's visits, I often shared my faith with her about how God had brought me through so many obstacles and scary times. I told her about my family at church and how they had helped and brought me through with much prayer and love. She listened and said she would like to come to one of the meetings with me. The Lord indeed works in mysterious ways!

8
New Life

Two years after the first transplant, when Tracey was eighteen, we received that very special call from the hospital again. We were all so excited, but this time Tracey was scared and unsure because she knew there was no certainty it would work, and she knew the procedure was going to be hard. However, we tried to reassure her that medical research had moved forward since her last transplant and now there were new surgery procedures and medication.

On arrival at the hospital, we waited for the nurses to collect us from the waiting room and carry out the normal checks. To pass the time, Vicky and Tracey were sitting in front of the vending machines looking at all the different chocolates and sweets. All we could hear was Tracey saying, 'I'm gonna try that one first, and then that one, and then that one...' She was so excited at the thought of eating chocolate freely.

When the nurse came to fetch us, I asked how long before Tracey would be going to theatre. She said that the kidney was on the way from Hereford. I remember thinking, 'Well, that's not as far as her last one – Bristol.'

The journey getting it to us may have been quicker, but this time the operation seemed a lot longer; we were all getting nervous.

When they brought her back from theatre, I was overjoyed as I looked at her. I knew the kidney was working because she had colour in her cheeks and her skin had a pink hue that had been missing before surgery. After a short while, the doctor came to see us. He was smiling and said that everything had gone well; the operation was a success.

We were all surprised at how quickly Tracey recovered from the operation; she was out of hospital in no time. She could eat and drink anything she wanted, and for the first time in her life she felt really well. We all take having well–functioning kidneys for granted, but it meant the world to Tracey; she could go for a wee! She thought it was wonderful to go into the ladies' toilets when she was out anywhere. Tracey always smiled as she reminded people never to underestimate being able to go for a wee. I will never forget those words! Tears streamed down our faces on several occasions as we watched her finally live. She wanted to do everything she had missed out on, including going on holidays abroad. Finally, she had the life she had been dreaming of.

However, in time, this new life also brought heartache and pain – in a different way. Tracey was very vulnerable and easily led. Through her illness she had been protected and had never seen the real world – especially at night-time. She changed and wanted to go out and experience a normal life. This was a change for me also, as I wanted to keep her in that cotton wool protection that had become such a big part of my life.

When Tracey brought her boyfriend to meet us for the first time, I was pleased for her, but also afraid for her. He had totally swept her off her feet and she was so happy and in love, but I was afraid of her getting hurt. There were arguments and tears, and I knew I had to change; I had to let her go, which was a new experience for me, and it was hard. Clive tried to help me; he could see the frustration and pain I was going through. This was a new way of being a mother and after a while I did learn to accept it.

I also had a new life, and I could do what I wanted and have time to myself. I looked for a part-time job and started to think of things other than illness. I found it strange at first but started to enjoy this new life. Soon, Tracey, at around twenty, and her partner were happy, married and furnishing their new home, enjoying this new adventure.

By now, Vicky was training to be a hairdresser. I loved watching her character changing. At one stage she wore vibrant eye make-up, brightly coloured lipstick, had red highlights in her hair and wore punk clothing. Suddenly she was all grown up, training for a career and going out with her punk boyfriend.

Later, she settled down and had our first grandson, Clive Junior, in April 1986. She was so young, and it was hard for her as she had to give up work and money was scarce. Although her partner worked hard, life was still a struggle. Clive Junior brought such a joy into the house, though. It was strange to see Vicky as a mother with the responsibility of a baby. Two years later Vicky had our second grandchild, a daughter called Collette, and that was to be her family – one boy and one girl.

One day, I was out shopping with Tracey when she said with excitement, 'Mum, I have something to tell you. I'm pregnant.' I felt sick and thought I was going to pass out! I was astonished because the doctors had said she could never have children owing to her renal failure and, to be honest, it was the last thing I ever thought about.

I was suddenly afraid again. I had quite taken to this carefree life and suddenly fear stepped back in. It was dangerous for her to get pregnant. I wanted to shout at her for putting her precious kidney and new life in danger. My thoughts once again started to run ahead with everything that could go wrong. This pregnancy could put pressure on the kidney, as the new kidney had been placed in the front of her tummy.

At that moment I didn't even want to look at her. My anger grew as we walked home. I thought about what her dad would say, and I felt angry with her partner, for being irresponsible. He had put my precious daughter's life at risk! Of course, it wasn't just him, but at the time I needed to point my anger somewhere. Most parents would be thrilled with this news, but not me. All I could think about was how dangerous it seemed.

When she attended her renal clinic and told the doctor she was pregnant, he looked at her cautiously and advised her of the danger. He talked her through all the options. Tracey asked if the baby would be in danger, and this was something the doctor could not answer fully. It seemed that the baby would likely be OK, so she said, 'Well, then, I'm having it.'

Over the next nine months she was back and forth to hospital and even had to be admitted on several occasions, as sometimes there were complications. During this time, so many thoughts crowded my mind, all the what ifs. The main one was, what if anything should go wrong and the baby had to grow up without a mother, like I did?

The sleepless nights started all over again. I could see no joy in her having this new baby. I was totally sick of hospitals, sick of nurses and sick of waiting in corridors. I just wanted her to have a life with no problems – that's what we had fought for during all those years.

It took me weeks to realise that it was not about me, but about what she wanted.

Despite my fears, Tracey carried the baby remarkably well and had our little granddaughter on 3rd August 1989 in the local hospital, so that the transplant doctors could keep her under observation. Our new little granddaughter was called Abbie. Tracey was amazing, and she was a wonderful mother! She was overjoyed, and I sensed that she had been given a new reason to live and something, or someone, else to fight for.

Fourteen months later she was giving birth again. It was another little girl, and they called her Rebekah. These two children should never have been medically possible; however, they would play a big part in Tracey fighting for her life, and I believe played a role in how many years she experienced this world.

Kidney mum op hope

A newspaper article covering yet another fundraising event Tracey was involved with after her transplant and the birth of both children.

9
New Work

Tracey had started her new life, and that left Clive and me free to start ours. We both enjoyed fishing, so this gave us time to spend together, relaxing. We had a small touring caravan, and most weekends we liked to travel to Evesham, in Worcestershire. We parked by the river and enjoyed every opportunity to fish. The smell of bacon cooking while we were fishing early in the mornings was special to us both. We would take time out to eat breakfast, then it was back to fishing, a hobby we shared with a passion. The feeling of freedom and time to share just being together, doing what we liked, was growing on us and we loved it. I was enjoying this new lifestyle.

I had started voluntary training on the Samaritans' helplines and worked through the night. The calls broadened my knowledge regarding the pain and hardship of many, yet I looked back to see how God had lifted me through so many similar situations. Again, this amazing new life was such an opportunity to see God's mercy, with life-changing experiences.

My brother Tony had started a small engineering business, and he asked Clive and me to set up a new branch in the West Midlands. We were apprehensive because it would mean giving up our current employment – Clive was a long-distance lorry driver and I was working in a local supermarket – so it was quite scary, as it was all new to us. We had no idea about business and management. Where would we start? However, after much thought we decided to take a chance and go for it; what harm was there in trying? We found it exciting as we looked for the premises that ticked all the boxes. We rented a small factory unit on a local business park, and I enjoyed working with my brother for three years.

However, as time passed, I started to lose interest and no longer enjoyed my work. After much prayer and some tears, I decided to leave and seek new employment. My husband continued to manage the business for a further nine years.

I was surprised when my pastor telephoned me to say that he had put my name forward to work at Christ for all Nations (CfaN).[7] I remember thinking how wonderful it would be to have a job doing the Lord's work, but realistically I knew they would not employ someone with no experience in that area! So I thought no more of it and continued to seek other employment.

I eagerly waited for the post each morning, hoping for at least one successful interview from all my applications. One day I heard the post arrive, and as I picked up the letters, I noticed one with the heading 'Christ for all Nations'. I was so eager to see what it said that as I tried

[7] See cfan.org.uk (accessed 6th September 2022). Ministry founded by Reinhard Bonnke and his wife, Anni. Today led by evangelist Daniel Kolenda.

to open it, I ripped part of the letter – which asked me to go for an interview! I was already nervous reading the letter and began questioning myself. How would I get through an interview with these nerves?

I prayed and talked calmly to myself, saying that I could only do my best and have confidence. Sadly, my pep talk didn't work, and the nervousness didn't ease.

On the day of the interview, I waited in a side room to be called into the office and, to my surprise, as I walked through the door, I suddenly felt a calmness come over me. I answered each question honestly and said I had practically no computer skills, but I would be willing to learn. My heart sank as I left the office. I truly felt I was too inexperienced for the position. As I walked out of the building, I noticed all the people working there looked so professional and were typing fast without looking at their keyboards.

Again, I waited for the post each morning. To my amazement, I was offered the position and was asked to start the following week! I found myself in a job I could only have dreamed of. I was working in a professional environment serving my King. How the Lord can and will use the weakest vessel!

On my first morning at the office, I was thrilled to find that at the start of every day all the staff gathered for a time of prayer. What a wonderful way to spend the first hour of the day. My role was essentially to register people from across the globe who wanted to attend our ongoing conferences and other missionary events. While the events took place, I would be with my co-workers at the frontline, meeting and greeting, signposting people to the right place and, most importantly, listening, supporting and praying with people.

At this point, the planning had started for the Birmingham Euro Fire Crusade in the main arena of the NEC Birmingham; a crusade that brought people together from all over the world for worship, prayer, teaching, evangelism, networking, meeting amazing people of all faiths and ages, and sharing wonderful testimonies of God's blessings in their lives. No two meetings were ever the same – each was different.

We had to temporarily transport some of our office equipment to the NEC Birmingham and work from a substitute office for the length of the crusade. Because of the distance from my home, I travelled to work each day with my colleague who was also my supervisor. I felt really privileged as I walked around with my picture on my special badge, with 'Christ for all Nations' printed across the top.

Each day I watched the Holy Spirit move within people's lives. I witnessed miracles and shared in the emotions of people who came from all over the world with different life experiences; it was life-changing for me to see the powerful work of God each day. Most days I was asked to pray for people who were experiencing pain in their lives and seeking the living God to take them through their painful journey. I felt I could relate, and it was a privilege to pray with them.

I know God had put me in this amazing job that showed me each day His great mercy, love and power. He was showing me more and more of His wonderful love to carry me through the painful future that lay ahead, teaching me and strengthening me. I was experiencing His presence, which built me and moulded me. Seeing first-hand that nothing was impossible for God[8] was the foundation of faith that I would lean on in the years to come.

I gained so much while working for CfaN. The team of evangelists led by Reinhard Bonnke, the prayer warrior Suzette Hattingh and many more powerful, faithful men and women of God played such a significant part in my spiritual development.

---

[8] See Matthew 19:26.

10
Unexpected Chain of Events

Tracey's journey of freedom after her transplant, and the birth of her children, was unfolding throughout the years that I was working for my brother and CfaN.

Tracey left the hospital still working through some minor complications after having Rebekah, her second daughter. Abbie, her eldest child, was now fourteen months old. Each day, a midwife visited to make sure that both mother and baby were doing well, owing to the health complications. However, unbeknown to anyone, one midwife would start an incredible and unexpected chain of events!

The midwife who was meant to be visiting Tracey called the office to say she would not be at work owing to sickness. Margaret was one of the midwives available that day, and after noticing on the work rota that there was a visit to be made to a young mum who had received a kidney transplant, she took an interest in Tracey. She asked her supervisor if she could cover that visit and received approval to add Tracey to her daily list.

She arrived to find a twenty-four-year-old mother who was struggling with health issues. While she did the usual medical checks on Rebekah, she spent time chatting to Tracey about her past life on dialysis and her transplant. Later that evening, when I visited Tracey, she mentioned how this new midwife had seemed to be interested in dates, times and the hospital where the transplant had taken place.

Tracey was not aware at the time, but after this visit, Margaret was on a mission. Talking to Tracey had stirred up a suspicion and she could not stop thinking about it. She started to make some enquiries; she could not let what she had learned go unquestioned. She decided to call the transplant coordinator to book an appointment to find out if her suspicion was correct.

It is important to know that, in those early days of organ donation, patients were not allowed to know the identity of the donors. Hospital procedure in this matter was a very grey area. Margaret could not get the information out of her mind; she knew in her heart that this young mother was the recipient of her late brother's kidney. All the dates, the times and the hospital added up. All the information that Tracey had given her matched the road accident in Hereford which had caused her brother's death.

A few weeks later, Tracey was on the radio, broadcasting with a transplant coordinator. She was answering questions about transplant as a way of raising awareness of the importance of organ donation. A lady named Betty called the show and started to ask quite a lot of questions. Tracey had a strange feeling as she spoke to Betty and wondered who this lady was, and why she felt so connected to her as she spoke about her late son. She wanted to find out more.

Tracey's heart was breaking for the lady as she talked about the loss of her son and the pain she had experienced. The more Betty spoke, the more Tracey wanted to find out just who she was.

Tracey was not to know that during the time between the home visit and the radio broadcast, Margaret was busy asking questions and could not ignore the information she had found out. She had approached the kidney transplant coordinator and told them she was sure she had found the recipient of her brother's kidney. The coordinator tried hard to put her off the whole idea of pushing for information as it was not hospital protocol, but nothing was going to put Margaret off – she was determined!

After many weeks of meetings and discussions with hospital managers, and with Tracey's consent, a meeting was arranged. I am sure that hearts were beating as the professionals officially confirmed that Tracey had indeed received her kidney from Margaret's late brother, and Betty and Eric's son, Andrew!

This sequence of events from an unscheduled, last-minute home visit to looking into the eyes of the family who had changed Tracey's life forever was something no one could have foreseen. Tracey was thrilled to be able to thank the family, who had carried out the wishes of their son. He had given her the most precious gift of life, freedom from a kidney machine and from suffering. He was the person who had also given her the opportunity to have her two children, which was an impossibility without a kidney.

Following this meeting, a wonderful story unfolded and relationships were built. We were so blessed to be able to meet Andrew's mother and father and all of his family.

Betty told us all about her wonderful son, who was only nineteen when he passed away, filling in parts of this caring young man's short life. Betty told us of the day Andrew had bought a motorbike. She and Eric were not overjoyed about that, but lovingly accepted the news of his newest purchase. It was good to listen and learn more about this lad who had so much love and compassion. Betty reminisced about how he loved exercise and playing outdoor sports, and how he looked after his body and ate healthily. She recalled the day that Andrew had come home carrying two donor cards and told his mum and dad his wishes, should anything ever happen to him. Andrew's thoughts were always on helping people, so carrying the donor card came as no surprise to his mum and dad; he was always doing something for someone.

Betty, with tears in her eyes, told us of that devastating day they received the phone call that Andrew had been involved in a serious road accident while he was a passenger in a car with some of his friends. On arriving at the hospital, they were informed of the severity of his injuries. Heartbreakingly, Andrew was not to recover, and his family, completely unselfishly, even in a time of deep shock and grief, gave permission for Andrew's organ donation wishes to be carried out.

While Andrew's family were suffering with overwhelming pain, sadness and loss, we had been overjoyed to receive the phone call that a kidney had become available. We knew nothing of their grief and, looking back, we never really thought about the implications around where the kidney was coming from. We were only thinking of what this meant for our daughter. When we received that wonderful call asking us to go to the hospital, we were full of joy and hope for the future with our daughter, while Andrew's parents faced pain and grief for their future without their much-loved son. Now our hearts were breaking for their loss, and we hope that the family know that we have thought about them and still think about Andrew and the gift he gave us. He will not be forgotten.

I honestly believe that it was no coincidence that Andrew's sister turned up that day to cover Tracey's home visit. God really is the God of the impossible!

Over the following years, Betty and Eric shared in the love of Abbie and Rebekah, even to calling them their grandchildren. They watched the children grow up, and Tracey, Abbie and Rebekah often visited them at home.

Betty could see first-hand the difference donor cards make to the lives of many who are on the transplant waiting list and, like her daughter Margaret, she set out on a mission, determined to give out 250,000 donor cards. Betty did not stop there. She thought she would go even further and, with her husband's help, she started fundraising for the many other needs of kidney patients. With funding, she completely refurbished the waiting room in the hospital, making it a comfortable place for patients to sit and wait, and spent the rest of her life as a great ambassador for renal patients.

I could never find a way to thank the family and express my feelings. I wrote a poem for them,[9] hoping it would show them more of how I felt. I gave Betty and Eric a copy of the poem and they were thrilled; they even had it framed and placed it on the wall over their fireplace.

---

[9] Included at the end of this book.

How great is our God! Out of all the people in the West Midlands and Birmingham area, only He could bring this midwife to Tracey's door! I believe that God wanted to give Betty, Eric and the family the gift of seeing what their son had done. They were able to know that their son's kidney had not only given life to three people – Tracey, Abbie, and Rebekah – but would also learn that Andrew had given new life to others, too, through the donation of his other kidney and heart.

Donor crusade by a tragic mother

Donor Card
I would like to help someone to live after my death

By BOB HAYWOOD

A Birmingham mother has started a one-woman crusade to help life-giving transplant operations — as a poignant tribute to the memory of her teenage son.

Mrs. Betty Marsh, of Ilford Head, Harborne, has pledged herself to distribute 250,000 donor cards following the death of her 19-year-old son, Andrew, after a road accident last October.

Andrew, the youngest of four children, was a super-fit athlete and international powerlifter. He died in Hereford District Hospital 26 hours after receiving a fractured skull in a two-car crash at Woofferton, near Ludlow.

He never regained consciousness.

Her son gave help to three

Nurse

Andrew had been a donor carrier and his organs helped to give a normal life to three people, a girl of 19 and a man of 31, who each received one of his kidneys, and a man of 40, who had a double cornea graft to enable him to see again.

Mrs. Marsh, a maternity unit nurse at Dudley Road Hospital, Birmingham, said: "To me, my son isn't dead. I am a Christian and I pray for Andrew. I also pray for the three people who are able to live because of Andrew's gift.

"I don't think that people fully realise the life of a young person. The tragedy is bad enough when someone like

Andrew dies. But other young people are dying needlessly because of a shortage of human organs for transplant.

"I would like to make a plea for all people to consider carrying donor cards."

Bus stops

Mrs. Marsh said that she wanted to distribute 250,000 donor cards — partly by topping up depleted supplies in shops and surgeries and by directly approaching would-be donors. She added: "I even stop people at bus stops."

Mr Bill Essex, transplant co-ordinator at the Queen Elizabeth Hospital, Birmingham, which is one of the country's three transplant centres, said: "We are grateful to Mrs. Marsh and are touched by her gesture.

"It is marvellous and so typical of West Midlanders."

Mrs. Betty Marsh, of Harborne, Birmingham, holds a picture of her son, 19-year-old Andrew Marsh, who died after a car accident. She plans to distribute 250,000 donor cards.

An advert in the local paper about Betty and her hope of getting everyone to sign up to be an organ donor.

11
Simon

The children were still very young when Tracey's marriage became troubled and ended in divorce. She moved out of the house she had lived in with Terence for several years and moved into a high-rise council flat. It was hard for her to bring up two young children on her own, although they still saw their dad on weekends, and had – and still have – a wonderful relationship with him.

By this point, her kidney was struggling, and she often felt very tired and weak. Clive and I tried to support her. She was going through so many mixed feelings and regrets about what had happened, but she tried hard to pull her life together and start again. Vicky spent hours with her, watching the pain and frustration she was going through. She tried to support her during her sad times and was always there for her. Eventually, Tracey settled into her new life of looking after the children alone.

After what seemed like years of hurt for both Tracey and her husband, the day came when she received her divorce papers. By this time, she was twenty-seven and showing signs of renal failure. Her blood results were not good. In my heart, I knew that this kidney was not going to last much longer.

One evening she was relaxing and watching TV while the children were in bed, when the doorbell rang, and there stood an old friend she had not seen for many years. She had a friend with her and introduced him as Simon. We were to later find out that Simon fell in love with Tracey from that first meeting! Tracey also thought about him often after that night and wished he would get in touch again.

She was busy getting the children to bed one night when the doorbell rang again, and there stood Simon. He had a very shy and kind personality, and from that night romantic feelings started to grow; within twelve months, they were married.

Months before the wedding, Clive had a long conversation with Simon over a beer at the local pub, lovingly saying that life with Tracey was going to be extremely hard and although she looked well now, she was very poorly, and her health would only get worse. He also talked about the fact that Tracey had two small children and she would need a lot of help in looking after them. However, no words could change Simon's mind or put him off a future with Tracey; he had fallen in love with her and the children.

On their wedding day, Tracey looked so well and beautiful. However, I knew Simon was going to have a very bumpy future and he would need a lot of patience, courage and support. Simon had never seen anyone with renal failure before and did not fully understand the toll it would take on her, and also on him.

Tracey and Simon, on their wedding day with Abbie and Rebekah.

Quite early in the marriage, Tracey began to show signs of renal failure again. I had seen the signs many times before, and once I started to notice them, my stomach began to churn and the sleepless nights returned. By this time Tracey, Simon and the girls were living in a council house just around the corner from me, which made it easy for me to pop in each day. I could see that she was worrying about feeling so lethargic and about her test results that showed her blood count was low. The doctors decided she would need yet another operation, this time a hysterectomy. However, while waiting for the procedure she continued to become very lethargic and found it hard to walk far. She became pale, with darkened patches around her eyes, and found it difficult to do even small jobs. Finally, her body started to swell, and she stopped passing urine. Her kidney had stopped working.

During Tracey's time as a patient in different hospitals, she had made many friends and gained a name for herself as someone who was caring and knowledgeable about renal failure, kidney machines and transplantation, as a result of all her past experiences. Most renal doctors knew who she was and respected her bubbly and fun character. She had lived through and fought battles when medical odds were against her, giving her a reputation for surviving and picking herself up.

Many times she would receive a phone call and go to visit patients in hospital, helping to reassure them, and if she thought something was not quite right, whether it was the treatment or their financial issues within the system, she fought their corner. Her life had taught her how to stand against some hospital standards and she was not slow in saying so. I recall one time when a nurse on the ward came to look at her wound after an operation. She bent over the bed and was ready to proceed with removing the dressing, when Tracey looked straight at her and asked if she had washed her hands. The nurse stopped, apologised and immediately washed her hands. Tracey did not tolerate any messing about!

Tracey inspired patients and their families to have strength and courage during their times of struggling, through her effervescent nature. Some patients would call her because they had just started dialysis and were afraid; she spent hours talking with and reassuring them, even if she was on the dialysis machine herself. Sadly, there were times when the doctors could do no more for them and she would receive phone calls with news that they had passed away. Each person was special to her in her walk through those fearful days. She remembered each one fondly and tried to attend all their funerals.

One friend was incredibly special to Tracey from her early days of dialysis at the East Birmingham Hospital, now the Heartlands Hospital, on the paediatric ward. Her name was Toni and they had both gone through years of pain and operations, restricted fluids and rubbish diets. Tracey loved her friend Toni dearly! They had a special bond and regularly phoned each other to share all that was going on in their lives. Sometimes they would laugh and sometimes they would cry; either way, they had each other to lean on as they both understood the impact of their illness. Toni was like Tracey – she lived for the day, and she never limited herself. The two of them would go that extra mile and strived to live their lives to the fullest, not allowing themselves to be held back by their circumstances. Tracey and the children loved to visit Toni at her parents' house in Wales as often as they could.

One day, Tracey received the call that she had always dreaded, and tearfully listened as she tried to take in what the caller was saying. Toni had been outside the hospital on her way to dialysis when she'd had a fatal heart attack right outside the door, so close to the help she needed. They had shared so much during the years, and at the young age of thirty-one, Toni was gone. For days, Tracey's feelings were all over the place. They had been such an inspiration to each other and to so many kidney patients all over the country, both so vivacious and fun-loving, even among such lifelong suffering. Tracey cried for days at the loss and, as she prepared for yet another funeral, she wrote this special poem to read out for her much-loved friend:

For You, Toni!

Oh, Father God, Tracey where does it end?
She is tired and hurting in need of a friend.
We had a special bond, Toni, and I,
All the times we have listened to each other cry.

But then, days later, on the phone again,
You would think we had never experienced
pain,
That is the way it was, you see,
I helped her, and she helped me.

Our loved ones suffer and are hurting too,
We feel so guilty for what we put them
through,
That's the way it was you see,
I helped her, and she helped me.

But now you're gone, and I feel so alone,
You're no longer there on the end of the phone.
But knowing you, you'd hate all the fuss,
You will make sure you are always here with
us.

I know you're better now, and free from pain,
And although I will never hear your voice again
I know you'll stay with me until the end,
I love you and miss you,
My strong, special friend.

While Tracey was dealing with losing Toni, her own condition was getting worse. She was back on dialysis and was transferred to the renal ward at New Cross Hospital, Wolverhampton, for specialist care. She had never been in this hospital before, so it felt strange and different. Simon stayed with her on the ward as she was struggling to get her dialysis under control; her body was not responding to her usual drugs and she was having adverse reactions to all the medication changes. However, Simon still had to work and also had the children to look after, so he knew he couldn't continue staying with her daily at the hospital.

After some weeks, Tracey began to win the fight back to health and came home from hospital. Her only thought was the children. However, she was not home long before she fell ill again and was readmitted. Oh, how well we knew this pattern.

On the same day that she was admitted I noticed some spots on Rebekah. We learned that she had chickenpox, which she then passed on to Abbie. Clive and I had to look after the children, as it could be fatal for Tracey to catch it, and Simon couldn't look after them owing to the risk of carrying it to Tracey in the hospital. For several nights, Clive and I stayed up with one in each bed because when one cried it would wake the other, with both of them having high temperatures and scratching at their spots.

Tracey came home after a few days and longed to care for the children. Chickenpox – being dangerous to renal patients, especially kidney transplant patients – could cause a kidney to be rejected. So Tracey was not allowed to see the girls for at least two weeks. All she could do was watch them play in our garden through a small hole in the fence. The children were in the garden playing one day when I heard a voice call through the fence, 'Mum, bring them closer so that I can see them without them knowing!' She knew that if they realised she was there they would cry for their mummy. I can still see her, crying and wanting to love them; it was heartbreaking and frustrating. This constant battle my daughter faced would not ease; there seemed to be no end.

Tracey had to drive to the renal unit three days a week at 7am for her dialysis. The children were so young, they just thought she was going to work. She would dialyse, come home, go straight to bed and get up before the children came home from school. However, there were days when we received calls to say that Tracey had to stay in hospital, and on those occasions the children would stay with me until Simon came home; he always wanted the children to stay with him at night.

Simon quickly learned all about the kidney machine, the blood results and Tracey's strict dietary needs. He also learned to cope with all her mood swings and pressures; he knew how to handle Tracey with such love and care. The more he faced, the more he proved he could handle the strain and I was so proud of him. I knew that God had answered my prayers and sent him to love her and look after her.

After a while, he could read her moods, and he was wonderful with the girls. He worked hard to pay all the bills and would do the shopping at night when Tracey and the children were in bed. He never could cope with housework, but I loved to do that, so we worked well as a team. Although by now they were six and seven years old, Abbie and Rebekah were taught from an early age to do certain jobs around the house to help their mum, as she couldn't do a lot physically. There are home videos that show her and Simon spending hours on the floor playing with the girls, making cards or helping them with homework. She was often too ill to stand and play, so she would sit on the floor.

Tracey worked hard at keeping the family happy and would never let the children think she was really ill. Of course, they did see how ill she was, but she set them a good example of walking through pain and choosing to find joy in all the things she could.

On dialysis days, when Tracey left early for the dialysis unit, I would walk around to her house at 6am to get the girls ready for school. If she was late getting on her machine, it would throw the day out for the other patients who had the afternoon and evening shifts, so she always had to be on time. Once she had left, the girls tried to make their beds, the daily washing was put in the machine and general tidying of the house was done, so that Tracey could go straight to bed when she came home after her treatment. On the way to school, we would have fun, sometimes singing our favourite songs. The children enjoyed school and Tracey would always help them learn at home by taking them through their homework.

There were great times when Simon came home from work to find a note pinned on the front door saying, 'You have to follow the clues to gain entry.' On one occasion, he had to go across the estate to Vicky's house to find the clue hidden under her toilet seat. It was so lovely to see them always full of fun and playing pranks on each other.

Dialysis became harder for Tracey with all the issues caused by long years of illness and treatment. Her blood pressure and fluid retention became a problem, and she became very poorly. She was older and not as strong as she had been, so it was not easy to have another fistula operation. The vein in her arm was getting weaker and the blood flow was not good. We needed a miracle.

It was at this time I was reminded of what I had heard Tracey say: 'When we wake each morning, we can make a choice: we can choose to be happy or choose to be miserable. Being miserable is not going to change anything, only make everyone else miserable as well. Choose to face the day with a smile and you will get one back.'

She trusted that God would find a way.

12
Fight for Life

Tracey was now attending a local private dialysis unit during the week, as well as the hospital regularly for her monthly clinics. It was at this renal unit that she met Owen, a shy, kind, gentle giant whose laugh was contagious, just like Tracey's. They dialysed next to each other on the ward and to pass time they would cause havoc with the nurses and patients, always finding something to have a giggle over. Four hours is a long time to have to stay still lying down, but Tracey and Owen never let themselves grow bored. It is surprising what tricks they found to play from their beds, and they quickly became known as the 'Troublesome Two' on the ward.

One of the most memorable moments from early in their friendship involved a simple birthday cake. What could go wrong there? Tracey found a big round stone, which she covered with marzipan, icing and cake decorations, to look like a beautiful birthday cake. She asked the nurse to place it on the trolley at the side of Owen's bed. After blowing out the candles, he was given the knife to cut into it. His face was a picture, and the laughter flooded the ward! She did the same another year, only this time with a 'sponge' cake (a bath sponge with icing over it that dipped in the middle when he put the knife in), and a 'fruit' cake which was bananas and oranges with their skins still on and icing over the top. Their pranks would bring laughter all over the ward! Over the years Owen and his wife became, and still are, close family friends and are much loved by us all.

On the very first day that Tracey attended the privately run renal unit, Owen was surprised to see her setting up her machine and putting her own needles in. She explained to him that she had been on home dialysis as a child and had had to do everything herself. He was amazed.

One of the problems with dialysis is all the sitting around in waiting rooms, especially when there are other patients who are also waiting to be connected to their machines. After a patient has finished their four-hour treatment, the machines have to be fitted with new lines and sterilised, which takes time, so patients can wait for a long while before they start their treatment.

Eventually, Tracey convinced Owen that he could set up his own machine and put in his own needles. Along with nursing staff, she encouraged and helped him to start his training. Six months later, he was completely independent, setting his machine up and putting his needles in.

Tracey also encouraged others on the ward to do the same. This was a great help to the nurses as it gave them time to spend on new patients.

Owen attended a church where he was known for his wonderful singing voice. Tracey often asked him to sing at some of the fundraising events that we put on (such as fish and chip suppers, evening entertainment and a Christmas fete), and people always said how beautiful he sounded. I believe their friendship was God-made because of where the friendship took them – Owen ended up on home dialysis, something he would not have been able to do as easily without Tracey's encouragement and training.

Tracey and Owen; they enjoyed a friendship that spanned more than twenty years.

It was autumn 1998 when that wonderful phone call from the transplant coordinator came for the third time. Once again, we went through all the preparation and mixed feelings.

This time was a little different; the children were older and needed more comfort; they asked more questions, and it was not always easy to give them answers. They were used to their mum going in and out of hospital, but this was different and they knew it.

Tracey and Simon sat in the side ward anxiously waiting for the results of the compatibility of the kidney test and the general blood test results. After what seemed like hours, the doctors said the kidney was a good match. Tracey was prepared for surgery and again we all waited for her to come out of theatre. The wait was full of mixed feelings and fear. Finally, we saw her being transferred from the theatre trolley into her bed on the ward and, thankfully, all looked well. Tears were flowing with relief when the doctor came and told us the operation had been a complete success. 'Thank You, God!' was all I could say.

When I visited Tracey on the ward a few days later, she was very agitated. I asked her what was wrong. She was worried that the staff who were attending to her didn't seem to have the right training for a renal ward. Tracey had not received her Heparin injection and she was upset as she knew about the specific treatment that should follow her operation.

Many times, I had felt that there was a shortage of nurses on the ward, and on several occasions I expressed my concern. I was angry and frustrated because the surgeons had done a brilliant job, but the follow-up care was not being carried out professionally, which could result in things going badly wrong. On a renal transplant ward, it is imperative that there is specialised follow-up care. Whatever the reason, whether it was owing to Tracey not having this special care, or something else, her kidney failed: our biggest fears came true again.

Tracey was rushed to theatre as the kidney had clotted and she was struggling and in pain, so it had to be removed quickly. Once again, she was fighting for her life. For days we sat by her bed as she fought and fought. I truly believed that she was not going to give up easily as she had so much to live for, with her girls and a loving husband. She would not give up without a fight! This was always what Tracey did: when she was at death's door, she fought her way back over and over again.

I remember standing in the hospital corridor, fuming. I could see no further than thinking it was the aftercare that had let her down. The kidney was good – it had been working perfectly. On so many occasions over the years, I had to keep quiet and smile because I was afraid of upsetting the nursing staff when I had to question treatment. I had learned doctors and nurses do make mistakes, and this time I was convinced it was nursing care. Even the doctor could not give a good reason for what had happened. Standing in that corridor, I felt there was no future. I was completely drained and felt I could take no more. 'Why is this happening?' I thought. There seemed no comfort at this time. Nothing made sense. My thoughts were completely confused and out of control.

I needed to go back into the ward, but I felt afraid. I knew my daughter needed me, but I was so helpless and felt God had let us down. I knew I had to get my daughter home, and smile, but how?

How was she going to go back on dialysis? How was she going to find the strength to fight the fear once again? I called out with so many questions, so much disappointment. I was angry with God, angry with the nurses...

Tracey returned from hospital and once again started dialysis. Her strength was fading, and I wondered how much more her body could take. Each day the anger and frustration became more intense as we watched her struggle. It was breaking Vicky's heart to see her so weak and in so much pain, as each movement was difficult.

A few weeks after Tracey came home from hospital, we received a letter from her consultant to make an appointment to see him; we knew it was not going to be good news. However, we were not expecting him to tell Tracey that she could never go back on the transplant list! She had too many antibodies from the previous transplants, and if given another kidney, her body would reject it as soon as it was transplanted. This meant she would spend the rest of her life on dialysis. We also knew it meant she would only have a short time to live because the dialysis and operations had taken their toll on her body. Her heart, lungs and joints had suffered because of continuous treatment. Tracey was silent. Simon tried to ask questions. No one else said a word. I can't remember leaving the room or anything else in those devastating moments.

As a family, we started to make the most of every day, trying to enjoy what little time we had, but it was so painful. Tracey became so tired, and everything was hard for her. I remember thinking about the future. My mind was running away with negative thoughts and fears; it started to make me ill.

Tracey had stopped attending church, owing to illness and many mixed feelings, struggles and disappointments. However, Abbie and Rebekah came with me each Sunday. One Sunday, to our surprise, Tracey said she would come with us to church. When we all arrived that morning, my church family were really pleased to see her. They had continually prayed for her over the years as she walked her painful journey. This Sunday morning was to be one that would stay in my heart.

Tracey was full of emotion throughout the service, then suddenly, during a silent time, she started to sing a chorus out loud. Everyone in the church sat in silence and listened to every word, feeling the emotions of the lyrics. The chorus was an old one we used to sing years ago, when Tracey and Vicky attended church with me as children. It's called 'Jesus, Take Me As I Am'.[10] The words in the song meant a lot to her as it was just how she felt at that time. I don't think there was a dry eye in the church.

I knew at that time she had opened her heart and allowed God in, fully, so that she could begin to heal. The journey she had walked over the years of pain, fear, frustration, disappointment and the loss of so many friends had taken its toll. Perhaps now God could start the deep healing, as He had done with me so many times.

Sometimes the mountains we face in life seem hard to start climbing; they look insurmountable, and it can be difficult to take that first step, but she needed the Lord to take her hand and help her start this new journey. Truthfully, Tracey's faith had wavered at times since she had been baptised, with unanswered prayers, which was hardly surprising.

---

[10] Dave Bryant, on *The Worship Collection*, ThankYou Music. See hymnary.org/text/jesus_take_me_as_i_am (accessed 7th September 2022).

The weeks following were difficult, as each day we were looking for signs of her health failing. We had no idea how to get through each day, what to say or how to stop showing our fear. One Sunday morning, a leader in the church was listening to me as I shared my feelings and worries for the months to come. He gave me these words that really comforted me: 'June, God cannot give you what you need, until you need it. Trust Him and He will take you through when the time comes.' In the past He had proven it time and time again. I just needed to be reminded by this faithful man of God.

Tracey always encouraged Abbie and Rebekah to see their father, Terence. Abbie and Rebekah were excited to be bridesmaids at their dad's wedding and they liked his new wife, Maria. They had their own bedroom at Terence's new house and spent some weekends there. The two families were friendly and always got on. Both families would come to birthday parties and other celebrations for the girls and were a solid unit of four, all raising the girls together. This friendship meant we could invite them all to church and family functions without any ill feeling; many people could never understand this, but we felt it was good for the children.

Tracey and Maria formed a special bond, and Tracey knew Maria genuinely loved the girls. There was never any bad talk on either side, only consideration and love for each parent.

Clive's mum, Nora, and I had also become like mother and daughter. A memorable time I had with her was after I had written a poem called 'The Cross', which she had framed and hung on the wall in her living room. While doing her housework one morning, I asked if she believed that Jesus was the Son of God. She said yes, and we started to have this wonderful time talking about her feelings about the Lord. She had never talked like this before and started to cry. She had gone to Sunday morning services with Tracey, the girls and me, and to many church functions, but had never shared her feelings until now. That morning we prayed, and she gave her heart to the Lord. We both cried with joy at that most precious moment.

13
Hope

Headlines began to appear in newspapers touting a new treatment for renal patients that had been pioneered in America. The headlines said that the new procedure had been tried on four people in the UK's East Midlands and had been a success! The treatment worked by removing antibodies from a kidney organ, which allowed a live donor to donate a kidney without the same level of risk of rejection, owing to antibodies – it was a big medical breakthrough. This was great news as it applied to Tracey's condition. It was because of incompatible antibodies from all the previous transplants that she could not have another kidney, and this new procedure could potentially be a way around that. My heart was racing as I read the article and I could feel that hope was already starting to emerge. I wanted – no, I *needed* – to know more.

After speaking to Tracey and Simon, with their permission I called to make an appointment with Tracey's consultant at the hospital she was attending. Equipped with the newspaper cutting, I asked if he would write to the consultant providing this new treatment to see if he would consider Tracey as a patient. At first, he was apprehensive and said it would do no good because of Tracey's history with previous transplants, but, after a long conversation, he said he would at least write and ask the question. I didn't say anything to anyone in case it came to nothing, but I fasted and prayed while I waited for a reply.

After what seemed like months, that special day came to meet with the doctor who would talk Tracey through the procedure. Simon was sitting beside Tracey in this small clinic while Abbie, Rebekah, Clive and I sat behind. We were nervous as we listened to all the questions he asked. Surprisingly, for a man so high in the medical research field – a leading consultant, physician and nephrologist[11] – he was easy to talk to. After he had looked through Tracey's records and asked many questions, we eagerly awaited his decision and were filled with joy when he said yes, he would consider her for the new treatment!

We all came out of that room with new hope. I felt like a huge cloud had lifted and wanted to pinch myself to make sure this was true. We had been sure that this chance would never come again and that we were near to losing Tracey, but maybe, just maybe, this would not be the case now.

It wasn't long after our meeting that he spoke the treasured words we all wanted to hear – she could receive another kidney!

We patiently waited each day for a phone call or a letter with some news. What was the next step for moving forward with this new, medically advanced procedure? My thoughts had already travelled a distance ahead and I

---

[11] Relating to matters of diseases affecting the kidneys.

was wondering who in the family was going to be the donor. Who would be a compatible match? Finally, the letter came, and tests began on all the family members, apart from Abbie and Rebekah.

My thoughts over the next few days were constantly on this new procedure and trying to believe that this was really going to happen. We carried on with our everyday lives, all the while waiting for a phone call. Each day that passed felt like an eternity, and I found my mind often wandered and I became impatient, waiting desperately to hear from the hospital.

Finally, I received a letter from the consultant asking me to attend a clinic as, for a second time, many years later, I had been found to be the closest match. I was so excited, I phoned Clive at work – and then Vicky. I was not expecting the response she gave. She was devastated and started crying. I had not realised how much she had wanted to be the one to give her sister a kidney.

As she was crying, my heart broke for her; how could I tell her that I was pleased she was not a match as she had a full life ahead of her? I felt I had lived much more of mine and she needed to be there for her children. Putting the phone down, I started to pray to get my head around the previous few minutes.

My prayers had been answered! I had been a match all those years ago but didn't give my kidney because a cadaveric kidney had become available. All these years later, with new medical advances and breakthroughs of procedures, some new anti-rejection drugs had been discovered. Yet again, I had the opportunity to give Tracey one of my kidneys. What a privilege! I had questioned God so many times over the years, asking why I could not give that first kidney. Was this the answer? Was this His timing?

Clive was apprehensive. After all, two people he loved so dearly, his wife and his daughter, were both going to be in the operating theatre at the same time. He had always been a wonderful support to us all, but who was his support now? It was so difficult for him.

Clive and I arrived at the Walsgrave Hospital, Coventry, for my first health tests. As we walked down the maze of corridors, following the signs, we found the echo heart scan[12] department. We covered all the tests over the next few weeks: heart, bloods, kidney function scans and chest X-rays.

During those days, the kidney transplant coordinators supported us all through each step of the journey. They were never too busy and always answered our questions. They would telephone me at home if they were not in the clinic at the time of my visit, if needed. I was amazed at how the full team worked together, from consultants to surgeons to transplant coordinators – every detail was in place, which alleviated my stress and took away any fear. They made time to explain everything and gave us confidence with their knowledge and happy, pleasant personalities.

Throughout the tests, I remember being really worried in case anything showed in my health that might stop this transplant going ahead, including my age as I was now sixty-four. However, to my relief, I was given the go-ahead and the date was set.

---

[12] The echocardiogram is a scan to look at the heart.

While testing me, they had also started Tracey's new pre-operation treatment. She had to go on dialysis as normal, three times a week, and on some days in between she would use another machine to remove her antibodies. We were told it may have some side effects and would make Tracey feel poorly for a short time after the treatment. Thankfully, she didn't experience these side effects, and everything seemed positive.

When the date was set and all details for the operation were put in place, I was scared in case I caught a cold or any other virus that might stop the transplant from happening. We were so close, and I was worried about losing this opportunity we had been waiting for. We were very aware that this could be Tracey's last chance of a transplant, as her health was diminishing.

It was September, which meant the cold and flu season was on the way, but I was determined not to pick up anything that would get in the way of this opportunity. I became obsessed with avoiding any crowded places, and kept myself locked away. I refused to use public transport, go shopping or visit people. I did not want to catch a cold!

14
A Miracle

When the day of admission came, Tracey and I both felt more relaxed than we had for weeks. I felt a peace that could only have come from God. I felt confident in the knowledge that we were in the hands of an excellent team. Over the previous months the doctor had been involved in many pre-surgery meetings, including nursing care and with transplant coordinators. He had explained to Tracey and me all that would happen, step by step. I knew that when I woke up after the operation, Tracey would be better. I just knew that God would bring us both through. This was His timing, and I had no fear at all about the operation, only excitement for what it meant for my daughter.

Vicky was trying to be strong for her dad, but just a few days before our admission she went down with a heavy cold. This meant that she could only look at us from a distance across the hospital foyer and, more importantly, she could not comfort or look after Clive at home in case he passed the virus on to us in hospital. She had tears streaming down her pale, drawn face, and I could see the fear in her eyes as she looked across the partition, unable to come any closer or give us a hug before we went into theatre.

Clive was strong and never showed his emotions until the nurses came to put us on the trolleys and wheel us down the corridor to the operating theatre. He kissed me and, as I looked at him, his expression said it all. He just broke down and couldn't be strong any longer. I will always remember the cry he gave as they wheeled me away. I had never seen my husband cry like that before.

Pastor Dave and his wife, Sandra, pastors of our church at the time, had come to pray with us before we went to theatre. I saw them both go to Clive, and I knew he would be OK with their support. My church family (and many other churches) were praying for us. As I approached the doors of the theatre, I said, 'Lord, it's all in Your hands now,' and, in a way, it was a great comfort because I didn't need to worry any more. The last thing I remember was counting: one, two, three…

When I was back on the ward, although very drowsy, I overheard the nurse say that both operations had been a success. I knew Clive was sitting by my bed and could hear nurses talking to him; however, I was unable to respond. I am not sure if it was the morphine that had been given to me as pain relief, but I felt as if I was asleep, although I could hear everything that was happening. To my amazement, I felt no pain.

The following morning, I was pleased to hear the doctors say that the kidney was working, and Tracey was doing well!

As I started my recovery it suddenly hit me that one of my kidneys was now Tracey's kidney and it gave her the freedom of new life. Throughout all the tests and hospital visits, I had never thought of it that way. What a wonderful privilege God had given me to give my daughter freedom from dialysis.

I was surprised, and grateful, that the pain of healing was not anywhere near as bad as I had expected. The aftercare on the ward for us both was excellent, and the nurses were all so pleasant. I could tell that the nurses knew exactly what they were doing. Their professionalism and happy attitude helped us to relax and heal. Just six days after the operation, I was in the car and on my way home.

Tracey had to stay in hospital for another month as she had a few problems. The new kidney struggled for a while, but the doctor and his amazing team of consultants were always on top of it. His professional knowledge helped to keep Tracey relaxed and she healed faster because she was not lying in her bed worrying about the kidney being rejected. Instead, she lay in her bed, reading books and giggling with the nurses, a sharp contrast to how she had been after her other transplants.

After leaving hospital, Tracey had to attend follow-up appointments. This meant a good hour's travel from home, but it was worth the effort as she had built friendships with the clinic nurses and doctors, and they supported her so well.

Over time, Tracey began to appreciate the personality of this wonderful surgeon who had saved her life. He always had the answer to any of the medical hiccups and problems that followed the transplant. The operation was only the first step; good medical follow-up was crucial for at least twelve months. During the time of her check-up clinics, the doctor learned to read Tracey's nature and personality, which was not surprising – he had been part of her pranks! Most of the renal nurses already knew her nature and were never surprised by some of the silly things she said and did. Many renal patients who attended the clinics talked to her and could see the strength in this lady who had walked through unchartered medical history. She was able to talk to them and understand their feelings.

Over the years of recovery, during Tracey's visits to clinic, the doctor asked if he could use some of her medical case notes as studies for the training of his new students, as there were so many uncommon issues that would help them in their future studies. During one clinic appointment, Tracey was surprised when a student doctor stood up to shake her hand, saying he was so pleased to meet her as she was considered a legend in their medical studies. He was one of the doctor's students and he already knew all about her amazing journey. It warms my heart to think that Tracey's medical records have helped train doctors to support patients in the future.

During the latter part of the first year after her fourth transplant, Tracey started to feel ill, and we couldn't understand why. The kidney wasn't doing well, and her health was failing, but there was no reason for this to be happening. After carrying out tests, the doctor said Tracey had developed an infection called cytomegalovirus (CMV). The medical symptoms are like a bad dose of the flu, but it is a more virulent virus and can be serious in someone with a transplant since the lungs, gut and bone marrow can be affected. Fortunately, new drugs to counteract CMV were effective, and Tracey responded to these. However, the infection can also induce rejection of the donated organ by stimulating the immune system.

The doctor sent Tracey for a biopsy that showed rejection, and even after using several different types of treatment, the kidney function steadily got worse. Then, another biopsy showed that she had a lymphoma, and it was serious.

The news left us completely stunned, as it was something that had never crossed our minds. Cancer was not something we had dealt with before or were prepared for. Here we were again, in a place of wondering. How many more knocks in life could we all take? We should have been reaping the joys and benefits of this new kidney.

The doctor took the only option he could to help Tracey fight the infections, which was to stop the anti-rejection treatment. This would put Angelica – the name we had given Tracey's kidney – in real trouble, but it would also help her fight infections. This was an unheard-of thing to do after a transplant; however, to even the doctor's amazement, everything gradually got better.

If you stop immunosuppression, a lymphoma will often go away as the body's immune system recovers, but it is usual for the kidney to then be rejected and fail completely. In Tracey's case, the kidney function kept getting better and the antibody level stayed low. In the end, she only needed a small dose of steroids to maintain her health.

After stopping her anti-rejection drug, Tracey was very anxious, so the doctor restarted her on a low dose; even though he knew it would essentially have no effect medically, he knew it certainly would psychologically.

Abbie and Rebekah both enjoyed the church youth group. They had a faith of their own, but Tracey was struggling. It was a Sunday evening, and the girls went with their youth leaders to a church service in Birmingham. Towards the end of the meeting, the pastor invited people who needed healing to come to the front for prayer. Abbie and Rebekah both said that they had such a strong feeling that if their mum had been there, God would have healed her. This was something that they had never experienced before, but they were not going to let it rest.

They asked their mum to go with them to the meeting the following week for healing, but Tracey refused. However, Abbie and Rebekah told their mum that giving up was simply not an option! They cried with her, they got angry with her and they persisted in telling her that this was a leap of faith she just needed to take. They didn't mince their words about how they felt about her refusing, and so she eventually gave in and went to the next meeting with them.

Tracey was prayed for at this healing meeting and returned to her seat. She told the girls that when she went for prayer (against her will!), she was praying to a God she didn't believe would heal her, and saying, 'Please heal me, not for my sake but for the sake of my girls. I don't want them to lose their mother and their faith at the same time.'

She repeated this over and over in her mind, and then described hearing the clear voice of God say to her, 'Why do you keep asking Me, when I've already done it?' Wow! Tracey had not heard the voice of God before, nor afterwards, I believe, but this was God telling her she was healed! The girls told Tracey that she didn't need to worry, and they all went for a curry!

A few weeks later, Tracey went for her regular tests at the clinic and was asked to come back for repeat tests as the results were wrong. After the second round of tests, the hospital called her, and she was told that the lymphoma had completely gone. Tracey had received no treatment for the lymphoma, only the change of treatment regarding her antirejection medication, so there was no explanation as to why it had gone. I believe it was a true miracle.

Tracey's kidney had taken a knock during those weeks and now it was thought it may only last a few more months owing to her current low dose of anti-rejection drugs. However, she stayed on that same dose of the drugs for years and Angelica (the kidney) got stronger and stronger, continuing to stay at a healthy level! This should not have been medically possible. It was lovely to live through, and to see the many treasured, happy and active years where Tracey made memories with her girls, family and friends.

As I look back over those months, I can see God's hand over everything; from God keeping my kidney for 'such a time as this'[13] to Tracey being healed of lymphoma. I thought I was too old at sixty-four to donate a kidney, but with God, nothing is impossible. He not only gave me a healthy body pre- and post-surgery, but He also gave me the best surgeons and hospital staff. The operation was on 10th September 2005 and each year, on that day, we celebrate, in honour of Angelica.

---

[13] Esther 4:14.

Tracey's life completely changed. She found she could do all the things she had always wanted to do again! She went on holidays abroad with the family, enjoyed eating and drinking all the different foods that she wanted, and she could walk without getting exhausted. She continued to make everything fun – her laughter was contagious – and she always had her daughters as cohorts to play pranks… usually on me. I was always wondering what the next trick would be, especially if Vicky was with them. I never knew what they would get up to!

On one occasion I came home from holiday to find *all* my cupboards, my shower, my microwave and even the cat's food bowl full to the brim with multicoloured pit balls, and the clock on the wall and all my fridge magnets turned upside down! These were only mild jokes; others were filmed and put on Facebook, and I'm told that Tracey and the girls started getting requests for more videos because people really laughed at them.

Abbie and Tracey were both youth leaders at the church during this time. It was soon recognised that the young people loved Tracey's cheerful ways, and they would often approach her if they had concerns in their lives. Her heart was for helping the young people, and her love for the Lord. She lived life to the fullest and enjoyed being free from dialysis; she touched the lives of many by being a witness to what God had done in her life, as well as showing tremendous courage and love for the Lord. Her faith had become really strong at this time and she was a great ambassador for the youth group.

15

Teamwork

These years were the preparation for my leadership skills and training for a change of direction. It was the start of a new ministry, although I was not aware of this at the time.

The church service had finished and Tracey, the girls and I were walking to the car, ready to go home. As we approached the gate to leave, I could see my sister Jean talking to Audrey, the then-pastor's wife. Jean called me over and asked me a question. My mouth said yes, in haste, while my head was saying no.

I had recently attended a council meeting regarding the new Disability Discrimination Act 2005, to be brought out by the government. This would have implications for our church building, as we only had outside toilets. I had been praying for someone in the fellowship to start a project to build a community hall extension to house internal toilets. I didn't know I would be the answer to my own prayers.

The church had been built in 1884 and needed continuous refurbishment. There were two toilets outside the main building in the church grounds, with steps to gain access, which prevented wheelchair access. There had also been several incidents over the winter months of people waiting outside in the rain and slipping on the ice.

Unbeknown to me, Jean had said to Audrey, 'Ask June to head the project; she's used to fundraising.' Years earlier I had, with Tracey and a team of people, headed some fundraising events to raise money to pay for holidays for kidney patients who were on dialysis, and to purchase machines and equipment for renal patients by holding fêtes, jumble sales and sponsored events. However, this new project was going to need hundreds of thousands of pounds, not to mention planning permission.

I was never academic. Nothing had changed as far as my letter-writing was concerned. For this reason, I thought about what I had said and went into a panic. I had said yes to filling in funding applications to send to secretaries of charitable trusts, something I knew nothing about.

The following Sunday, I planned to go to Audrey and say I had changed my mind as it would be too much for me. However, partway through the service, John Bedford, our pastor at that time, called me to the front of the church and said, 'Would everyone please stand? We are all going to pray for June, as she has agreed to head the building project, to provide internal toilets.'

As I walked to the front of the church with my legs shaking, no one could have known my thoughts. As John prayed, I never heard a word, I was so deep in thought: how could I get out of this?

Some weeks later, after agonising at home, I was told about someone at our sister church who was also seeking funds for a similar project. I picked up the phone and called her. We had quite a long conversation and said we would work together. This was the start of a great friendship. Together we signed up to attend some training classes.

The first class brought back the struggling feelings of schooldays when I couldn't take everything in. Later that evening I found myself praying, 'Lord, I just cannot do this.'

A few days later, after attending a class, I asked the tutor if I could have a word with her and I explained that I had no idea where to start with the project. She advised me to start by forming a management team to help with the planning. Wow, that sounded great, as I would no longer feel that I was on my own! I prayed, and God supplied my needs. I approached eight other church members who I thought would commit to the project, including the church treasurer.

The first meeting started with prayer for the Lord's guidance throughout the whole project. We agreed that we would be called the Acorn Team,[14] because from a small acorn grows a mighty oak tree, and at that time I felt like a very small acorn indeed! In time, as the meetings progressed, I started to grow excited as each one in the team shared their thoughts about the project.

I continued to go to training days with more confidence. After spending days filling in funding

---

[14] Phil Langford: fully qualified building surveyor; Brian Collett: electrician; Peter Wilkes: plumber; Joan Nicholson: church treasurer; Yvonne Wilkes: admin (she wrote the minutes for each meeting); Jean Holliday: planning fêtes and other money-making activities; Mavis Jukes: helped with everything – she had a great gift for design and interior décor; David Woodhall and myself.

application forms, I would send them to Tracey to proofread. She noted all my mistakes in red marker pen, and put my commas and full stops in the correct places! When she returned them, the whole application forms seemed to be covered with red marks.

During her years on dialysis all she could do was read, so she was perfect as my proofreader. I testified at several churches how she was my Aaron; in the Bible we read that God provided Aaron to help Moses because of his speech problems,[15] and it was wonderful to have Tracey improve my writing and spelling.

After receiving many refusals, I became despondent and wondered if one of my applications was ever going to be accepted. Tracey tried to encourage me, but I was getting more downhearted at every refusal. Throughout this time, God blessed me through Tracey; she was never too busy and always gave me confidence that I could do this. But I knew I was doing something wrong.

I started to pray as I sat at my desk in the bedroom, which had now become my office. I cried out, 'What am I doing wrong, Lord?'

I don't know if I can explain what happened during that prayer time, but I truly felt as if the Lord was leaning over my shoulder and encouraging me to write from my heart; to write with the passion I had for the project and to stop using jargon. I followed this encouragement, using *my* words and not following all the teachings of the tutor. I also prayed over the application as I completed it, and again when I put it into the post box.

---

[15] See Exodus 4:10-16.

It was Saturday morning when a letter dropped onto my front door mat. As I reached to pick it up, I recognised the charity name on the envelope and knew it was a response to one of my applications. My hands were shaking, not wanting another refusal. I started to read the letter, but then noticed a cheque inside for £4,000. I jumped up and down and ran around the living room, shouting, 'Thank You, Lord! Thank You, Lord!'

That was the start of many successful applications. Once I started to use my own words, God stepped in and gave His blessing. He had given me a wonderful opportunity, and what came through that in the future was amazing, as it was the start of my journey towards gaining a reputation for fundraising. I was later offered jobs around raising funds, and it was a good foundation for becoming a 'learning champion'.

I will never forget the day I arrived at the church to see the building contractors spreading the concrete for the foundations. My thoughts were, 'It is really happening!' We started building, although at that time the full cost for the project had not yet been reached. By faith, we continued to build wall by wall and area by area – and the pot (as we called it) never emptied.

Towards the end of the first year, to fully meet all the costs, we needed £50,000. I had sent out an application for that amount and was still awaiting an answer.

Then my friend with whom I had attended the training classes telephoned me, and her voice was full of excitement. She had received a cheque from a charitable trust for £50,000. I was doing my best to give her my encouragement, and I was really pleased for her, but at the same time, under my breath, I was saying, 'Lord, that is what we need to complete our project, £50,000! Would You please bless my last application?'

Some weeks later, a letter dropped through the door from the charitable trust I had sent an application to, and there was a cheque inside for £5,000. I put it on the shelf in the lounge with the letter and hurried out to do my shopping.

Later that morning, on returning from work, my husband noticed the letter and the cheque. He phoned to congratulate me, saying, 'Well done, June, I see you've received the cheque you needed for £50,000.'

I said, 'No, it's £5,000!'

He said, 'June, did you have your glasses on when you looked at the cheque? Because it's £50,000.' God had provided yet again!

The community hall was completed, and all the funds had been provided in just over twelve months. This included a ladies' and gents' toilet, disabled toilets and a new fully fitted commercial kitchen, plus a general office for the pastor and secretary. The building was fitted with central heating and was carpeted throughout, with plenty of storage room.

With the community hall finished, the Acorn Team could reflect on what we had accomplished and how this project had helped us to work together, each using the gifts God had given us. This reminded us of the scripture in 1 Corinthians 12, which talks about the Church as a body, a unit, made up of 'many parts' (v12). And this was not the end for me or the Acorn Team, as there was an endless need for funding for all the projects we started in the community hall. There was an infinite demand for group equipment. Writing applications for funding seemed to never end, but I began to truly enjoy it.

Over this time of seeking funding, I gained quite a reputation and found myself being invited to help with planning community workshops and participating in community projects. To my surprise, through word of mouth I was contacted by a worker at Sandwell Council and offered the position of a learning champion. It was a job I loved, as it was working with community projects. I could visit any project within my set boundary. This meant I could encourage the leaders to seek funding to enhance their ongoing projects, or help to plan new projects, enabling me to meet some lovely people. It was a perfect opportunity for me to show the 'Jesus in me' that I loved.

Amazing things happened, giving me opportunities to pray for people and share my testimony. I was invited to speak at ladies' afternoon groups – it was such a privilege. God's plan started to fall into place, and I was reminded of the lady who had handed me that leaflet many years before, and how it had changed my life. We never know how many hearts we may have touched.

I was surprised, and deeply honoured, when I received a letter from the council, inviting me to the yearly awards celebration. This was an occasion to buy a new outfit and I was looking forward to the evening. Clive and I were greeted at the entrance and escorted to the table which had our names on place cards. I was amazed to see that the person giving the awards was the BBC TV presenter Michael Collie.

As the evening was coming to an end, my name was called to go forward and receive the 'Citizen of the Year' award. I nearly fell from my chair, as it was one of the greatest honours of the evening; somehow, I had received an award for doing what I loved!

Tracey came up with a plan for the church youth groups; she wanted to use the old manse in the church grounds for breakfast and after-school clubs. She asked, 'Mum, can you get funds to refurbish the house for after-school homework and activities?' Once again, the Acorn Team sprang into action. Tracey's enthusiasm for the project flowed over to the youth, who organised car washes, tabletop sales, sponsored events and even shovelled snow to raise money.

The plans for the building were to include a general office. Tracey excitedly chose a place for her desk, and the treasurer and church secretary would share the same office. There was even a place for Socks, Tracey's goldfish. One of the larger bedrooms was to be fitted with desks for the computers, and a general meeting room. The plans included a kitchen with microwave and toaster, and a large disabled toilet.

The old manse was completed and fully equipped, and it was all brought in through charitable trust funding. Preparations were made for the opening day, and the Mayor of Sandwell cut the ceremonial ribbon. The press were also invited.

However, Tracey, the person who had had the vision for it, was missing. She never sat at the desk, and she never entered the finished building.

16
The Next Journey

Tracey turned to me one morning in 2016 and light-heartedly said, 'Mumma, the doctors have asked me to go to Walsgrave Hospital in Coventry for a brain scan. I think they want to see if it's still there.' My thoughts drifted to a few weeks earlier, when she had mentioned how she was getting very forgetful and was losing her sense of smell and taste. It had happened so quickly, and now she could not even smell perfume, so I knew something was wrong.

She had been seeing a memory doctor for some months prior to this, who visited her at home. On one occasion, the doctor asked if I could be present at the consultation. At first, I thought this was strange, but after listening during the session I realised why she had wanted someone there. Tracey struggled with many of the simple questions. She could not recall questions after a break or remember basic facts that many would find easy. It was the memory doctor who requested the scan, based on these symptoms. I realised something was wrong and started to wonder what it could be. I hoped that it was simply because of all the morphine and other drugs that she had been given over the years.

She received a letter to attend the hospital for a brain scan, and shortly after, the results came back with minimal concern. Tracey joked about being relieved they had even found a brain, let alone a normal-looking one! The scan showed that there was some calcification – a condition characterised by abnormal deposits of calcium in the blood vessels in her brain – but this was sometimes common in renal failure patients, so nothing was thought of it.

Yet as time passed, we started to notice small changes in her health, and she became increasingly tired and forgetful. However, she never complained and just carried on each day as usual, not taking much notice of the symptoms. After all, she was now nearly fifty years old, and it was normal for her to get tired and to lack energy.

One evening in early 2016, Abbie came home from work extremely excited. She told her mum and the rest of the family that she had been accepted to lead a group of volunteers, which meant spending three months in Brazil, working with an anti-human-trafficking charity. This type of work was exactly what Abbie had wanted and felt called to do. However, it was not straightforward as she would have to fund the journey herself, at a cost of around £2,500. She had been considering for some time leaving her job working with Youth for Christ.[16] She could have asked for an extended break but felt she had gone as far as she could in this job, and was ready for a new challenge and a new journey in life. So, tearfully, she handed in her

---

[16] A Christian charity that provides support and guidance for young people. See www.yfci.org (accessed 7th September 2022).

resignation at work to plan for this amazing opportunity abroad.

Leaving this role to go to Brazil was a huge leap of faith, as not only did she need to meet the cost of the journey, but she also didn't have any certainty of work when she returned. The scripture found in Philippians 4:19, 'And my God will meet all your needs according to the riches of his glory in Christ Jesus', came true for Abbie at that time, as the church gave her *three parts of the money* as a gift, and the rest came in via donations within a month. It was clear that this trip was part of God's plan for her.

Abbie was flying out from London Heathrow on 1st May 2016. Tracey, Clive and I drove her to the airport, singing and laughing all the way. Shortly after we arrived in the departure lounge, we found the rest of the team that she would be spending the next three months with, getting to know each other. They were all mixed ages and just as full of excitement as she was. As one of the team leaders, Abbie was caught up straight away with setting plans into motion. We could see that she was busy, so we each gave her a tight hug and said our goodbyes before starting on our journey home, sad and missing her already.

Tracey had tears in her eyes as we left the airport, as this would be the longest time she had ever been away from Abbie. She willed the three months to pass quickly and was already planning her welcome home!

During those next three months, Tracey kept herself busy in the church office, dealing with paperwork for the youth club and planning future events and activities. There were plans and dates to be made for fundraising events, youth trips, safeguarding workshops and parents' evenings. She loved leading the youth group and supporting the young people who came, so it was no trouble for her.

We all laughed the day she walked into the church office with a goldfish. Humorously, we looked at each other to see who was going to ask the next question. Tracey explained that this was the new office goldfish, whose name was Socks. We asked why she called it Socks, and she chuckled and said, 'Because he has no feet!' It didn't make any sense at all, which made us chuckle even more. Socks quickly became a legend in the office, and each time Tracey was in hospital, a rota was made for people to feed him. I think he was the best looked after goldfish in the world.

As I mentioned earlier, after having her scan, Tracey started to show signs of illness. Some examples were mild headaches and physical changes, such as her eyes sinking back into their sockets with dark patches around them, which meant she looked ill most of the time. We were all still on a countdown for Abbie's return and were even more keen for it after reading the blogs that she posted weekly; they showed how amazing, but also dangerous, the work in Brazil was.

During the time Abbie was away, Rebekah moved from her apartment in Rugby, where she had been living for two years, back into our local area, so she could be closer to her mum and to the new job she had secured. We were all so proud of her for getting the position! She found an apartment just ten minutes from Tracey's house. Simon worked away from home at the weekends, from Friday to Monday morning, so Rebekah coming back when she did was perfect timing, as it meant she could pop in on her mum during the weekends and help her, now that she was starting to feel ill again. I am sure Tracey treasured those moments they spent together.

Then, before we knew it, the time was drawing near for Abbie's return, with just a few days to go. Tracey had made silver and pink banners to take to the airport; everyone was so excited for that arrival day to come! But then Tracey was handed a bitter blow. The day before Abbie was due home, she had the first visible symptoms of what was to be the start of her next journey.

The night before Abbie's return, Tracey was at home with Rebekah when she had a nosebleed. Rebekah went to get tissues, but things quickly escalated, and it became apparent that this was not a normal nosebleed.

There was no stopping the bleeding so Rebekah called 999 for an ambulance. However, she used the word 'nosebleed', and she was told an ambulance would not come out for a nosebleed. She tried to explain that it wasn't just a normal nosebleed – there were pools of blood, and her mum was about to pass out.

Rebekah couldn't drive her mum's car so she called Clive and me; in her frustration she was so angry and couldn't understand how they could leave her and her mum in such a vulnerable situation.

I will never forget the pool of blood that was in the living room and trailing into the kitchen, with tissues covering it. I was so thankful that Rebekah was with her that day and that Tracey did not have to be alone at such a scary time.

After leaving the hospital, I returned to the house to clean up the pools of blood.

Tracey had waited so long for that day to pick Abbie up from the airport, but sadly, as the plane landed, she lay in a hospital bed.

When she arrived at the hospital, they used two excruciatingly painful plugs to stop the nosebleed. Throughout the process of inserting the plugs, Tracey was screaming for them to stop. Rebekah was so brave and stayed with her mum even though it was traumatic. She felt really helpless at hearing her mum screaming and asking them to stop; it was so heartbreaking and terrifying for her to watch.

Owing to the severity of the bleed, the doctors insisted that Tracey should stay on the ward overnight. The nosebleed lasted for two days, and when she finally came home, she was looking very pale and had bruises on her face from the pressure of the plugs. She was relieved to be home and to finally be able to hear all about Abbie's trip. She was so proud of her.

This nosebleed should have alerted the doctors that something was wrong, but unfortunately it was not followed up.

17
Revisiting the T-junction

Re-store me, O Lord,
Life is weighing me down and I'm amid
darkness,
I feel afraid, beaten, alone; this mountain is just
too high.
I stumble.[17]

So many times, during these next chapters, I revisited the T-junction sign I mentioned earlier – when I could see a straight road stretching ahead, and at the end of the road was a T-junction with a sign pointing to the right: 'Follow and trust Me,' and to the left: 'Walk in anger without Me.'

I needed to restore my faith as so many emotions clouded my mind. My faith was being tested.

On 16th August 2016, Tracey phoned me early in the morning and cheerfully told me that she was on her way to hospital for another head scan. She said it was just a follow-up, and that Abbie was taking her, so I had nothing to worry about and she would see me later.

---

[17] My own poem.

The day was passing, and I didn't think anything of it. It wasn't until I had a call from Abbie in the afternoon that I knew something was wrong.

Abbie told me they were admitting Tracey into hospital, as the scan had shown a mass on her brain. I could hear the panic in her voice as she proceeded to tell me what had happened. To pass time while waiting for the scan, they were sitting doing a magazine puzzle together. Then Tracey left Abbie to finish it alone while she had her X-ray.

Tracey was out again in less than fifteen minutes and told Abbie that the doctor wanted to speak to her. Abbie knew instantly that this meant something was terribly wrong. The doctor told her that they would need to go straight to A&E to speak to a more senior doctor. He could not give them any more information, but by his tone, Abbie sensed there was a serious problem.

They were soon waiting in a side room as different doctors came and gave their opinion, some saying it was serious and some saying it was not. After what seemed like hours, Tracey was admitted to a ward for further tests. They had left for the hospital at 5.30am and Abbie did not leave her mum's side until just after midnight, when the hospital told her she had to leave.

That night, Tracey was taken to a private room in the neuroscience ward of the hospital and waited for two long weeks before they were able to do a biopsy. I will never forget the doctor coming to draw an arrow on the side of her neck with a marker pen, to show where the biopsy was to be taken. They knew the mass was at the top of her nose, travelling back into her head, but they did not know what it was.

When they brought her back to the ward after the procedure, both of her eyes were black. She had packing in and around her nose, held in place by a sling from ear to ear that was resting under her nose. She couldn't eat or drink without it getting in the way.

Following the biopsy, she had a constant flow of a strange, clear, watery substance running from her nose, which she would chuckle about and say that her brain was leaking. She had to keep wiping it away and simply said, 'Excuse my brain juice,' when people were around. I couldn't believe that she was still finding things to laugh about while sitting in a neuroscience ward with a mass in her head.

About a week after the biopsy, she was moved to the oncology ward, which we were confused about as no one had told us why they were moving her. Why were they taking her to the cancer ward? We were completely in the dark. We had been asking for days but were always told that the results were unclear and needed to be tested again. It was such a frustrating time.

Simon and Abbie were visiting Tracey when a doctor entered the room to bring the frightening report that the mass was cancerous.

No one wanted to be the first to speak. What do you say after hearing something like that? Eventually Tracey said, 'Well, at least now I know what I'm fighting.'

I could not believe it when I heard the news. I had been hopeful, as some doctors had been saying it was nothing serious, so this was a hard blow; my daughter had a cancerous tumour in her brain. This was nothing like what we had faced before!

What would I say to her?

What would I say to Abbie and Rebekah, Vicky and the rest of the family? How would I, as a mother, wife and grandmother, react to this news? I wanted to shut myself in a room, kick doors, throw things, shout at the top of my voice, 'Why?' and make it all go away. I had to compose myself.

Two weeks later, Tracey came home with an appointment to attend the oncology clinic. The family was invited to attend as well, so Simon, Abbie and Rebekah went along. As the day approached, they were all nervous and didn't know what to expect.

The specialist opened the conversation, introduced herself and proceeded to inform them that Tracey's condition was very serious. The type of tumour she had was a rare one – only 3 per cent of all cancers. The doctor showed them the scans of the tumour and they could not believe its size. It was 4cm wide and 8cm long, starting from the bridge of her nose and going up through the base of her brain. How did this not have more symptoms?

It was going to be a difficult battle for her. The specialist told her that, because of how complicated this tumour was, they were still trying to figure out the best approach. We later learned that various specialists had been debating and discussing it; some believed an operation would kill Tracey, but others recognised that she would die shortly without an operation anyway. The specialist told her that regardless of what the plan was, it would involve some sort of radiation treatment, so she should start eating well and exercising to prepare her body for what it was about to go through. She told her that she needed to put on some weight as she would lose it through the treatment.

Tracey was given another appointment to be told her final options. This time, Clive and I went along with Tracey, Simon and the girls. There were four specialists in the room at the clinic – an ear, nose and throat surgeon, a neurosurgeon, a top cancer specialist and a nurse – and we were told that surgery was the only option. The specialists had attended several meetings over the weeks to agree on the best procedure, which explained all the waiting around we had been doing.

It was decided that they would go ahead with the operation, as without it she would only have a matter of months to live anyway, and they wanted to give her as much time as possible. They continued to explain that the cancer was close to her left eye, meaning they may not be able to save the eye and may have to remove it, so her recovery would be painful and extensive.

My brain could take no more. I could see their lips moving but could hear no sound as I looked across the room to see my daughter sitting in a wheelchair next to Simon, showing no emotion. My heart was breaking as I watched her being put in this position again, facing immeasurable pain and countless operations, with her life hanging in the balance. We had walked through kidney operations over many years, and we knew the terminology and procedures. This brain tumour was devastating new ground, with lots of dark areas that we could not understand. She was given an operation date for the following week.

Tracey had built such a full life for herself; she was like a breath of fresh air when she entered a room, and was always laughing and full of fun. My heart was crying, 'Why? Why? I do not understand, Lord!' I was broken, and a mess every moment of every day following that meeting. I felt as if my heart was in anguish, and no number of words from friends could help me understand, or ease my pain. Each night, I lay awake wondering if she was afraid and what she was thinking. Clive tried to support me, but he himself was broken. I lay wondering what was going through the two girls' minds. Were they crying? Was Tracey crying? Then there was Simon, Vicky and the grandchildren to worry about, as well. My brain was running wild and there were no answers. Until the nosebleed, there had been very few symptoms. The few that she did have, such as the calcification in her brain and the memory loss, just happened to coincide with symptoms from her past years of renal failure, so were put down to being in relation to that.

During the final meeting, closer to the day of the surgery, the senior cancer specialists talked us through the steps that Tracey would need to follow to prepare, including taking medication to prevent fits, owing to the placement of the tumour. When we came out from the consultation, everyone found it difficult to say anything. We were all stunned by what we had just experienced.

Tracey carried on as cheerfully as ever and took the opportunity to eat and eat and pile on loads of weight. She and Abbie went out every day, and Rebekah joined them on the weekends when she wasn't working.

It was coming up to Halloween when all this was happening. Tracey was giggling to herself one night. Abbie asked what she was laughing at, and Tracey said that if she lost her eye, she would be able to scare all the trick-or-treaters who came to the door.

Because she chose to enjoy each day, she gave us all a feeling of hope. She was still making plans for her future and never spoke of negative thoughts. She carried on playing jokes on me, including soaking me with water and tricking me into asking a shopkeeper to pay for my parking. Anyone who didn't know her would never have guessed she was about to have such a serious operation.

18
The Final Battle

Tracey was admitted into hospital on Monday 10th October 2016, to await her operation the following morning. That evening, after unpacking her clothes and settling into her room, Simon asked the ward nurse if he could take her out to have a meal with the family. The ward nurse was very understanding and gave him permission, so we all went to a local place for some good old-fashioned pub grub. Tracey sat at the head of the long table in the restaurant with all her family and close friends around her. She looked so radiant and was laughing with us all as she ate a full rack of ribs! Even after finishing her plateful, she had her eyes glued on everyone else's food, ready to demolish any leftovers.

At the end of the evening, in the restaurant car park, Tracey hugged and kissed us, and cheerfully said she would see us the next day, after the operation. She showed no fear and shed no tears. It was about 9.30pm when she left to go back to the ward. I held her so tightly in my arms that night in the car park, never wanting to let go.

On the morning of her surgery, there was so much traffic. The hospital was roughly an hour away, but it took us much longer to get there. Abbie's satnav had taken her off the motorway to avoid traffic, thankfully, so she was able to spend more time with her mum that morning. But Clive, Simon and I were only able to spend twenty minutes with her before the anaesthetist arrived. He came into the room to explain his part of the procedure, along with a renal doctor who would be in the operating room to make sure the surgeons did everything they could to save Angelica, her precious transplanted kidney. Angelica was an added complication, as the operation and treatment methods for the tumour would threaten the kidney, which the doctors were keen to avoid.

The theatre staff came into the ward with their special caps on, and my stomach churned in fear. They told us it was time to go, and Tracey stood up to give us all a hug and kiss. I didn't, in all honesty, believe this would be the last time I would gaze into those beautiful, kind eyes and see that brave, loving smile. At that time of holding her, it was like my mind and body separated and everything closed down; I didn't know how to feel. I had to be brave for her, but it felt as if everything wasn't happening. Now as I look back, I believe the experience was God helping me to walk that moment in time.

Tracey still didn't cry or show any fear. She simply hopped onto the theatre trolley and said, 'See you all later,' as she was wheeled into surgery. As I turned and looked into the faces of the family, a feeling of all-over numbness swamped me. Their faces said it all.

We were all advised to go home, as when she returned from surgery she would be very tired and would need rest. The operation that we thought would take four hours turned into eight. We were relieved to receive the call that

Tracey was in recovery. Abbie – who wasn't working at this point – had stayed at the hospital the whole time, waiting for news, and was told that Tracey had come through the operation. The surgeons were pleased with the results, and said they believed they had removed *most* of the tumour. They even believed that no damage had been caused, despite the tumour being further into the brain than they had originally thought.

Simon drove back to the hospital, and he and Abbie went in to see Tracey, but she was still unconscious from the operation, so they didn't stay.

The following morning, we were told that Tracey had woken up and she knew her name and where she was. All seemed to be positive, so they moved her out of critical care and into a post-surgery ward.

Simon and Abbie went to visit her the next morning. Rebekah wanted to be with them, but she had taken so much time off that she could not ask for more. She had to try to concentrate on work while waiting in anticipation for a phone call, praying for some good news.

The following day, arriving at the hospital as soon as they were allowed to visit, Simon and Abbie could see Tracey was only semiconscious. She was responsive through blinking and squeezing their hands, but she was unable to talk. The doctor came to update them. He said Tracey was making good progress, so they both stayed a short time and then left so that she would sleep. Abbie shared with us all later that evening that the last thing Tracey did was squeeze her hand when she asked if she loved her. Oh, how Rebekah would have loved to have been there at that moment.

Late that night, Simon had a phone call from the hospital. We had all been on a high, relieved that everything had gone so well and were looking forward to improvement. But with this telephone call, we quickly came crashing down with the heart-stopping news that Tracey had suffered a stroke. She'd had a bleed in her brain, and they needed to take her back into surgery to relieve the pressure. Simon was advised not to go to the hospital as he wouldn't be able to see her, but to come first thing in the morning. Simon, Abbie and Rebekah shared the difficult task of telephoning family members in the early hours of the morning, and all agreed to set out early the next day.

We were on the motorway when the surgeon called and told us that he was sorry, but Tracey was back in critical care, and she was showing no response in her eyes. He would not say it over the phone, but he was suggesting that Tracey was brain dead.

I looked at her in that hospital bed, attached to a life support machine, in an induced coma, and all I wanted to do was wrap my arms around her to make her feel safe and know she was not alone; just to hear her say, 'Uvu, Mumma,' which was her special way of saying, 'Love you, Mumma.' Sadly, I could not touch her because of the risk of infection. She was surrounded by all these machines and special bedding that was like bubble wrap, only much bigger, to keep her warm. I asked myself, 'Is she aware of what is going on around her? Can she hear us?' But there was no way to know. My heart cried, 'Please, please let me love her and let me hold her just once more!'

We were told that they were unsure what damage had been done by the stroke and that there would be no way to know until they were able to wake her. We clung on to hope. Tracey lay in this coma for two weeks, and during this time, things would change; one moment we were told she was doing well and the next we were told she would not make it through the day. It was exhausting. No day was plain sailing and there were always new complications arising.

After the first week it was decided by the doctors that they would try to wake her, and we were all buzzing with expectancy. The wonderful news was sent across the internet to all family and friends that Tracey was going to be awakened today.

We all gathered in the waiting room ready for her to wake up and took it in turns to sit with her when the medication was reduced, waiting for her to open her eyes. Abbie sat by her bed and was desperate to see some movement. She came running out of the ward at one point, full of excitement, saying that she had seen her mum yawn, hoping this meant she would be waking soon, only for her hopes to be shattered, on returning to Tracey's bedside, to find her unchanged. The doctors were there and gave the sad news that Tracey was not responding, so they had increased the sedation medication again.

Afterwards I asked the nurse about the yawn. She said that it was simply Tracey gagging on the tube in her throat.

Over those two weeks, we learned the names of all the specialist nurses on the rota who cared for Tracey. They showed such kindness and helped us through our pain as we walked the highs and lows. Abbie and Rebekah were given a writing book and pen by one of the nurses who could see their pain as they sat with their mum; she told them to get people to write in it daily, like a diary for Tracey to read when she woke up. The entries were varied, from updates on her condition to updates on TV programmes she loved.

Tracey had visitors from the renal ward staff who had treated her over the years; they were very supportive whenever they came to see her and the family. It was precious to see how much they all cared.

As I walked into the critical care unit one day, I could see Vicky and Clive Junior sitting at the side of her bed and noticed their paleness and drawn features. Vicky's face told a story of heartbreak as she watched over her sister. I asked myself again why my family was going through so much hurt, disappointment and fear.

I was surprised to see that Tracey had been connected to a dialysis machine, which made me feel sick in my stomach. I knew that if she was aware of what was going on she would be upset, as Angelica was so precious to her. When I questioned the nurse, she said Angelica was struggling a little, so they were taking some of the strain off her, but she was still working and holding her own.

By this point, Tracey had caught an infection, but the hospital staff were unable to identify where it was coming from or what the infection was. They were trying various treatments but were struggling to fix it. The infection was causing problems with Tracey's blood and organ functions. She was already weak, and this was the last thing she needed. She had been on a low dose of anti-rejection medication for her kidney since the day she had her transplant, which left her open to infection. Doctors now had to decide whether to remove the anti-rejection medication altogether, to allow Tracey more chance of fighting the infection but lose the kidney, or to carry on with the medication and keep her vulnerable to infection but preserve the kidney. No one really knew what to do.

In her final week, it just so happened that most of the family were at the hospital when we were told that Tracey had had a second brain bleed. A neurosurgeon called us into a room and told us that they needed to rush her to theatre again to reopen the wound, and it was likely she would not survive the operation; the words no family wants to hear.

We were also told that if she did somehow survive, she would not be the same person we knew, as the damage caused to her brain during this bleed was extensive. We were able to go and say goodbye quickly before they took her to theatre, and we were horrified to see how swollen and bruised her head had become. We were given permission to kiss her as the risk of infection was now irrelevant, given that she was not expected to return.

All the family sat patiently waiting all night in the critical care waiting room, expecting the worst news. Tracey was gone for three hours, and it was an excruciating wait.

Once again, my daughter defied all the odds and pulled through the operation! Her fight never gave up, even in the coma, which was giving us hope that she would overcome all the odds and recover.

For the entire time she was in the coma, we waited and hoped that she would open her eyes; each day we looked for change, until the day Simon called us all to say the doctors wanted to see the family.

As soon as they walked us into that dreaded room, we knew that it was bad news. We had seen so many families go in there during our visits and come out crying. We named it the 'bad news room'. One of the doctors said that, unfortunately, Tracey had sepsis and was not responding to any medication or making any improvements.

They could do no more to help her and they would be turning off the life support machines that day. It is never easy for these decisions to be made; however, they were focusing on doing the best for Tracey, to preserve her dignity in death.

You could sense the awkwardness of the two doctors as they expressed their sympathy and left us to take it all in. They had become quite fond of Tracey, with one nurse commenting that although she had never met her awake, she knew she liked her from all she had heard about her. The silence only lasted a moment before there was a huge cry.

Abbie and Simon left the room to call various family members, so they could come to the hospital and say goodbye. Pastor Dave had come to the hospital, and he went to see Tracey and prayed for her.

Within an hour, there were loads of us there and I remember looking across the room to see Tracey's friend Sean hugging Rose, his wife, and daughter, Gemma, in a state of shock. Terence, Tracey's first husband, came with his wife, Maria, to comfort the girls and say goodbye to Tracey. Vicky had her head on my lap and was crying uncontrollably. I looked at Abbie, Rebekah and Simon, and did not know what to do.

How do I walk this final journey, Lord, that You have spared me from so many times, that has shadowed my life for so many years?

This was final. I wouldn't laugh and enjoy any more good times with my wonderful, kind, happy daughter.

The doctors turned off the machines and told us it would likely be a short time before Tracey passed away. I was holding on to the hope of one more miracle as I sat with her. The family took it in turns to sit at the side of her bed. The short time the doctors predicted turned into eight hours. She was still defying the odds! Angelica was still playing her part until the very end.

Tracey looked so peaceful, as if she was only sleeping. Abbie had her head resting at the side of Tracey's head saying, 'I'm here, Mumma, I'm here, don't be scared, I'm not leaving you.' She told her mum that the Bible says she had a room waiting for her in heaven[18] and asked her to reserve the one next door for her to move into. She told her to paint it pink and get it ready.

It is said that the hearing is the last thing to go before someone dies, so I believe Tracey would have known we were all there for her as we spoke to her the whole time. I sang her songs from childhood and told her how much I loved her.

Tracey slipped into the arms of the God she loved on 28th October 2016 at 11.40pm, surrounded by her family, who were clinging on to her hands, arms, legs and anything else we could get hold of.

No one could have prepared me for the feelings I would have as I watched my little girl fade away. I had

---

[18] John 14:2-3.

looked at Abbie, Rebekah and Simon, and known there was nothing I could say or do to prepare them for those last hours. I have never felt so heartbroken and useless as I did when I watched my precious daughter peacefully slip into her final rest.

After Tracey had passed away, the nurse asked if we would like a chaplain to come and pray for her. We said yes, and in what seemed like minutes, a kind chaplain came and suggested we all held hands in a circle around Tracey's bed. The chaplain said such a beautiful prayer and I remember thinking at the time that this was what Tracey would have wanted; all the people she loved were there and we prayed over her and said our goodbyes.

We walked from the ward to the car park. Clive started the car with tears so full in his eyes that he could hardly see. We couldn't talk through the one-hour drive home. My thoughts through part of the journey were that Tracey would never have to make that one- or sometimes two-hour drive to the clinic again, worrying about tests and wondering if her kidney was failing, as she had for the last several years. No more needles and operations, or pain, or suffering; it should have been a comfort, but I just wanted her back.

19
Celebration of Life

It was a few weeks later that a terrible thought entered my mind. I realised I had overlooked a promise I had made to Tracey many years earlier. I had promised to never let her stay on a life support machine, and this now bothered me. It was on my mind most of the time. One day I mentioned it to Simon, and he said he had also made the same promise. However, he was told by the doctor at the time of putting her on the machine that the doctor's decision can overrule ours, as they must do what is best for the patient. This helped us both as it was out of our hands. I was pleased I had shared my concern with Simon, as we were both feeling the same kind of guilt.

Simon also shared with me what Tracey had told him weeks before, after speaking to the surgeons. She said that she was not going to come through this operation, and that he must rebuild his life. But she never once showed this belief to the family.

To the very end of her life, Tracey knew her God and she had no fear of death. She knew her heavenly Father, she knew Jesus as her Lord and Saviour, and she knew His Word. Abbie had taken her mum for lunch prior to the operation and asked if she was scared. She simply replied, 'No. If I live, I get more time with my family here, and if I die, I get time with my Father in heaven. What is there to be afraid of?'

Simon, Abbie, Rebekah and Vicky threw themselves into the arrangements for Tracey's 'Celebration of Life'. We decided to call Tracey's final hours with us a 'Celebration of Life' instead of a funeral, as we wanted to celebrate all that Tracey was. She had made her arrangements years earlier, so plans were made around her wishes. Vicky and her daughter, Collette, went to the funeral parlour and did a beautiful job of doing Tracey's hair and make-up. This wasn't easy as the brain operation had taken all her hair from the front part of her head, but they wrapped a silver head scarf around the area of the operation so that it couldn't be seen. As I look back, I realise the pain they both must have gone through.

The celebration was well attended, with more than 400 people packed inside and outside the church, and there was a video link of the celebration to accommodate everyone outside the hall. Tracey had always wanted people to wear colour rather than the traditional black; she loved the sunset colours, and it was so beautiful to walk into the church and see colour everywhere.

Before arriving at the church, the funeral cars did a detour to George Road Community Church. Sadly, George Road Church was too small for the celebration, but it was special to be able to take my daughter there one last time. We all surrounded the casket and held hands to say a few words before we headed to our sister church, King's Community Church, where Tracey and Vicky had been baptised, and we had all spent so many hours and made so many special friends. I recalled for a moment just a few memories of Pastor Arthur Colman baptising them, and the way they both loved and served the Lord – even though Tracey did have her ups and downs! – and the happy times when, with the youth group, they enjoyed some amazing events. I could not think of a more special place she would have wanted to be for those last moments.

Pastor Matt Knott and his wife, Laura, greeted us and prepared the church and were such a comfort to us all that day. The celebration included some of Tracey's favourite songs and a prominent place for Socks, her goldfish, in his tank on the platform. There was a short message from our former pastor Dave Woodall, and so many happy memories shared by Simon, Abbie and Vicky. Rebekah was so traumatised she found it hard to speak. Our dear friend Owen tried to sing a song Tracey loved, but he just broke down in tears and could not sing. She would not have wanted this to be a sad occasion, so people filled their talks with funny stories that made everyone laugh.

The amount of love in the room was undeniable, and so many people spoke to the immediate family about how Tracey had touched their lives. There were messages from strangers across social media who had been following the story, each saying how Tracey had inspired them, even though they had never met her! She had such a unique way of touching lives; she was selfless and truly invested in love for others, and her legacy was clear from the words that were spoken to us on that day.

She was a woman with incredible strength, bravery and a determination to fight for life and embrace everything that it came with. She experienced such hardship and suffered immeasurably, but chose to use that to help others, and faced everything with a smile. The eleven years before she died she had good health, which meant we had ten wonderful years of memory-making. We will be forever grateful for that.

God had carried Tracey and given her a most wonderful gift, and He allowed me to be part of that walk. The greatest gift I could give my daughter came at the time God chose. There are still questions I ask myself to this day, at the age of eighty-one. However, I rest in the knowledge that all will be answered when I meet my Father, when He calls me home.

How will I end her life story when I know there is so much I have missed? Perhaps with the poem I wrote for Betty and Eric about their amazing son, Andrew, who donated his kidneys and gave Tracey her first chance of living life to the fullest, and allowing her to celebrate the two wonderful children she never thought she could have.

We never know why there is suffering. No one has that answer, but one thing I do know is I would not have liked to face it without my Father God.

20
Safe in His Hands

Let us then approach God's throne of grace
with confidence, so that we may receive mercy
and find grace to help us in our time of need.
(Hebrews 4:16)

Through these years, my daughter Vicky walked her own journey supporting her son, Clive, and her daughter, Collette, through both good and tough times. She was often the shoulder for Tracey to cry on, and a listening ear. They shared fashion and raided each other's wardrobes, as sisters do. Vicky was Tracey's confidence-keeper and her favourite ally in prank planning.

I started my memories from the year 1941. However, I believe my life truly started with a simple leaflet given to me by a lady in 1972, whom I have never seen since. But I still do wonder, was she an angel?[19]

I struggled with how to end this book, as there have been so many incredible chapters during my journey, in which I have questioned why Tracey walked such a

---

[19] See Hebrews 13:2.

painful life. Suffering can sweeten us, or poison and embitter us; either way, we have a choice.

I believe Jesus helped and guided us through those painful years. He walked with the family, giving us strength. I am amazed that each time Tracey's journey changed direction, God also gave me a new challenge. He always put me in a place of achievement and encouraged me. The Bible says in Isaiah 54:2: 'Enlarge the place of your tent, stretch your tent curtains wide, do not hold back; lengthen your cords, strengthen your stakes.' He always gave me a passion and encouragement when He started me on a new journey and a new season.

Tracey said to Abbie, 'If I live, I get more time with my family here, and if I die, I get time with my Father in heaven.' *Either way, there was a prize at the end.*

I look at the advancement in kidney research today and it amazes me. I see more clearly the confusion the doctors must have faced without the knowledge they have today. I am so thankful for the medical advancements, and the determination and training of new doctors. I am also pleased that Tracey was able to help to broaden that knowledge, through her history of treatment in extraordinary circumstances,[20] by allowing her medical notes to be used to help them improve even more. They are making new discoveries in kidney research, just as with many other illnesses.

It's not until all this time later that I have been able to understand the frustration the doctors must have endured when trying to diagnose Tracey's condition in those early

---

[20] Including renal rickets as a child, which followed her through her adult life, plus heart problems.

years. The answers were just not there in their medical journals. She often looked healthy, and she was still passing water – these are just two symptoms that would frustrate the diagnosis. Medical science has taken away many of the fears of kidney machines and transplantation as they are so improved. I can look back now and see that our frustrations were not because of incompetence; it was simply that medical science was not advanced in those days. Progress in these fields allowed the family another eleven years to enjoy with Tracey, time that was so precious.

My Father blessed us with those years and carried us through as we needed it. I was once told that God could not give us what we needed until we actually needed it. That is so true, as through these final years of my life I realise I have felt no anger at losing Tracey, only a joy that God gave me fifty years to love her. He gave me the precious gift of two daughters and an amazing husband. These past years I have enjoyed my grandchildren and great-grandchildren, who have all played a huge role in my walk as I have written about our journey.

I cannot begin to answer why bad things happen, but I hope some of the words in this book will help you to walk your own personal journey with the Lord. If you don't yet know Him, He is not far away. In desperate situations, perhaps you too will see the T-junction and allow God to help. Once I made that decision to trust and follow Him, He walked me through the highs and lows that we all face. His hand will stretch across the void; we just need to hold on to it.

The Precious Gift

The poem I wrote for Betty and Eric Marsh, kidney donor
Andrew's parents.

Who is this lad, who gave so much in life?
Who is this lad, who gave my Tracey back her
life?
Releasing her from the slavery of a kidney
machine,
Giving back the smile, that so long had not been
seen,
Freedom from those needles, in her veins day
by day.
Fluid and food restrictions, she could eat and
drink away,
She can walk and run and not feel tired.
Finally have the holiday her heart had long
desired.

If only I could thank him, perhaps I will one
day.
I can only tell my Lord and God, each morning
as I pray.
This stranger gave his only gift, as his life was
snatched away.

The gift that made it possible for my
grandchildren, here today.
He gave new hope and courage, to those on
kidney machines.
Proving transplants can really work, and the
happiness it brings.
How do you say 'thank you' to a mum and dad
who feel such pain?
No words could ever say enough, all would be
in vain.

Andrew Marsh – Donor.

Photographs

Family photos

*(Vicky's Son) Clive Cheshire and wife Debbie with
children Holly, Nicholas, Anthony.*

*Vicky's daughter Collette Buck with husband Ashley,
son Elijah and daughter Esther Rose.*

Simon, Tracey's husband, with Tracey.

Abbie, Tracey, Simon, Rebekah.

Tracey's friend Toni.

Front row: Mum and Dad Clive
Back row: Vicky and grandchildren Clive Junior,
Collette, Abbie, Rebekah.

Vicky, Clive, June, Tracey.

Vicky and Tracey.

Fundraising photos

*London Bridges walk for the Kidney Patients Association
Tracey, Rose (Sean's wife), June's sister Jean.*

Rose and Sean.

Tracey and June raising funds skydiving for Kidney Patients Association.

Sponsored Event for the Kidney Patients Association: George Road Community Church fellowship walking the Seven Bridges of London.

Teamwork photos (chapter 15)

The two outside toilets.

The new community hall.

The new community hall.

Two Acorn Team ladies, Jean Holliday and Yvonne Wilkes, cooking breakfast for the community and enjoying the newly built kitchen.

Joan Nicholson, Acorn Team treasurer.

Phil Langford, building planner and surveyor.

Peter Wilkes, Yvonne Wilkes, Brian Collette; front: Jean Holliday.

George Road Church.

Acknowledgements

My husband Clive Whitehouse for his support and encouragement over the years.

To my daughter Tracey, who inspired me to write the biography.

My son-in-law Simon, who carried Tracey through the good and bad days. He was her rock, always understanding, listening, compassionate and a wonderful father.

My daughter Vicky, who walked the journey day by day, sharing the laughter and the tears; she made that invisible little girl shine in all our lives, giving love, support, comfort.

To my granddaughters Abbie, Rebekah, and husband Nathan, for their editing and motivation to complete the manuscript.

My grandson Clive Junior and granddaughter Collette. Always there when needed, joining in Tracey's pranks.

My sister Jean. She was my confidence keeper, who always had a listening ear.

Sean, Rose and daughter Gemma. Faithful family always on call, and ready to give support; nothing was too much for them to do. We are blessed to have them as part of our family.

The renal staff at Walsgrave Coventry, for their loving care of Tracey.

To Andrew Marsh who gave the precious life-changing gift of his kidney with the consent of his generous and selfless family. A gift that gave hope to many on the transplant waiting list and made it possible for Tracey to have my grandchildren through kidney donation.

To Mr/Professor Higgins who played a role in Tracey's life, in the field of pioneering medical breakthrough, of transplantation.

Pastor John and Audrey Bedford. They had the vision for the building project.

To my editor Sheila and the team from Instant Apostle who walked me step by step through the publishing process.

Chapter 15: The Acorn Team
The team worked tirelessly on the building of the community hall and the refurbishment of the manse that was renamed Hope House.

Keith Burns, the contractor who built the community hall. He also refurbished the old manse/Hope House. He gave expert advice and finished the work in the timescale agreed.

The team
Phil Langford, building planner and surveyor
Joan Nicholson, treasurer
Pastor Dave Woodall
Brian Collett, trade electrician
Yvonne Wilkes, admin, including keeping minutes
Peter Wilkes, trade plumber
Jean Holliday, community fundraiser
Mavis Jukes, interior decor planner and all-round support